Pre and Post Competition Muscle Building Recipes for Bodybuilding:

Recover faster and improve your performance by feeding your body powerful muscle building and fat shredding meals

By Joseph Correa

Certified Sports Nutritionist

ACKNOWLEDGEMENTS

The realization and success of this book could not have been possible without my family.

Pre and Post Competition Muscle Building Recipes for Bodybuilding:

Recover faster and improve your performance by feeding your body powerful muscle building and fat shredding meals

By Joseph Correa

Certified Sports Nutritionist

CONTENTS

ABOUT THE AUTHOR

As a certified sports nutritionist and professional athlete, I firmly believe that proper nutrition will help you reach your goals faster and effectively. My knowledge and experience has helped me live healthier throughout the years and which I have shared with family and friends. The more you know about eating and drinking healthier, the sooner you will want to change your life and eating habits.

Being successful in controlling your weight is important as it will improve all aspects of your life.

Nutrition is a key part in the process of getting in better shape and that's what this book is all about.

INTRODUCTION

Pre and Post Competition Muscle Building Recipes for Bodybuilding will help you increase the amount of protein you consume before and after competing which will allow you muscles to recover and grow.

These meals will help increase muscle in an organized manner by adding healthy portions of protein to your diet. Not feeding your body properly before competition and cause you to perform negatively simply because of lack of strength and energy which are vital to do your best. Eating and nourishing your body after competition can have an even greater effect on your future performances and to your muscles healthy development.

This book will help you to:

-Gain muscle fast naturally when you need it the most.

-Improve muscle recovery right after training or competing.

-Have more energy.

-Naturally accelerate Your Metabolism to build more muscle.

-Improve your digestive system.

Joseph Correa is a certified sports nutritionist.

PRE-COMPETITION SHAKES FOR BODYBUILDING

1. Tomato protein shake:

Ingredients:

1 glass of skim milk

¼ tsp of cinnamon

1 small tomato

1 grated carrot

1 tsp of brown sugar

Preparation:

Wash and cut tomato into small cubes. Peel and grate the carrot. You want to cut the carrot into thin strips. Mix the ingredients in a blender and keep in the refrigerator.

Nutritional values for 1 glass:

Carbohydrates 10.9g

Sugar 7.85g

Protein 4.38g

Total fat 2.31g

Sodium 84mg

Potassium 423mg

Calcium 283.7mg

Iron 0.832mg

Vitamins (Vitamin C total ascorbic acid; B-6; B-12; Folate-DFE; A-RAE; A-IU; E-alpha-tocopherol; D; D-D2+D3; Thianin; Niacin)

Calories 80

2. Vegetable protein shake

Ingredients:

1 cup of chopped broccoli

half bunch of fresh spinach

½ cup of low fat yogurt

1 tsp of honey

few leaves of mint

¼ cup of water

Preparation:

Wash the vegetables and put into a blender. Put some ice cubes and blend together until smooth mixture.

Nutritional values for 1 glass:

Carbohydrates 12.32g

Sugar 7.16g

Protein 4.95g

Total fat 2.78g

Sodium 79mg

Potassium 243.6mg

Calcium 117mg

Iron 2.65mg

Vitamins (Vitamin C total ascorbic acid; B-6; B-12; Folate-DFE; A-RAE; A-IU; E-alpha-tocopherol; D; D-D2+D3; K-phylloquinone; Thianin; Riboflavin; Niacin)

Calories 81.3

3. Mixed fruits and vegetables protein shake

Ingredients:

1 cup of mixed blueberries, raspberries, blackberries and strawberries

½ cup of chopped baby spinach

2 egg whites

½ cup of low fat yogurt

1.5 glass of water

Preparation:

Wash the baby spinach and put it in a blender. Mix 2 egg whites with low fat yogurt, add water and put in a blender. Add mixed fruits and mix for few minutes.

Nutritional values for 1 glass:

Carbohydrates 11.27g

Sugar 8.11g

Protein 5.85g

Total fat 2.94g

Sodium 85mg

Potassium 259.6mg

Calcium 113mg

Iron 2.03mg

Vitamins (Vitamin C total ascorbic acid; B-6; B-12; Folate-DFE; A-RAE; A-IU; E-alpha-tocopherol; D; D-D2+D3; K-phylloquinone; Thianin; Riboflavin; Niacin)

Calories 72.6

4. Melon protein shake

Ingredients:

¼ cup of fresh strawberries

¼ of banana

1 slice of melon

½ tsp of cinnamon

¼ cup of chopped walnuts

1 tsp of brown sugar

Preparation:

Mix ingredients in a blender and sprinkle with cinnamon. Keep in the refrigerator and serve cold.

Nutritional values for 1 glass:

Carbohydrates 13.24g

Sugar 9.19g

Protein 7.92g

Total fat 3.54g

Sodium 91mg

Potassium 273.6mg

Calcium 119mg

Iron 2.09mg

Vitamins (Vitamin C total ascorbic acid; B-6; B-12; Folate-DFE; A-RAE; A-IU; E-alpha-tocopherol; D; D-D2+D3; K-phylloquinone; Thianin; Riboflavin; Niacin)

Calories 78

5. Strawberries protein shake:

Ingredients:

1 cup of strawberries

½ cup of skim milk

1 tsp of agave syrup

Preparation:

Mix the ingredients in a blender for few minutes. Leave it in the refrigerator for few minutes and serve cold. You can add some ice cubes in it.

Nutritional values for 1 glass:

Carbohydrates 8.19g

Sugar 4.05g

Protein 4.97g

Total fat 2.64g

Sodium 62mg

Potassium 197.9mg

Calcium 111mg

Iron 1.23mg

Vitamins (Vitamin C; B-6; B-12; E-alpha-tocopherol; D; D-D2+D3; K-phylloquinone; Thianin; Riboflavin; Niacin)

Calories 54

6. Vanilla protein shake

Ingredients:

1 glass of skim milk

½ glass of water

1 tsp of vanilla extract

1 tsp of minced vanilla

¼ tsp of cinnamon

2 tsp of brown sugar

Preparation:

Mix the milk with water and boil on a low temperature. Add minced vanilla and vanilla extract. Stir well and let it boil for about a minute. Remove from the heath and allow it to cool. Mix with another ingredients in a blender for few minutes. Serve cold.

Nutritional values for 1 glass:

Carbohydrates 10.12g

Sugar 6.05g

Protein 4.66g

Total fat 1.65g

Sodium 79mg

Potassium 203.4mg

Calcium 92mg

Iron 1.98mg

Vitamins (Vitamin C total ascorbic acid; B-6; B-12; Folate-DFE; A-RAE; A-IU; D; D-D2+D3; K-phylloquinone; Thianin; Riboflavin; Niacin)

Calories 79

7. Broccoli protein shake

Ingredients:

1 cup of cooked broccoli

1 glass of water

1 cup of goji berries

1 tsp of brown sugar

Preparation:

Mix the ingredients in a blender for few minutes. Serve this healthy drink cold.

Nutritional values for 1 glass:

Carbohydrates 9.31g

Sugar 5.19g

Protein 4.83g

Total fat 1.67g

Sodium 78mg

Potassium 201mg

Calcium 86mg

Iron 1.13mg

Vitamins (Vitamin C total ascorbic acid; B-6; B-12; A-RAE; A-IU; D; D-D2+D3; K-phylloquinone; Thianin; Riboflavin; Niacin)

Calories 68.3

8. Coffee protein shake

Ingredients:

1 cup of unsweetened chilled coffee

½ cup of skim milk

2 tsp of vanilla extract

2 tsp of brown sugar

1 tbsp of Greek yogurt

cinnamon (optional).

Preparation:

Combine all the ingredients in a blender. Mix well for about 30 seconds. Drink cold. You can add some cinnamon on top, but this is optional. Keep this protein shake in the refrigerator, or you can even freeze it for later use.

Nutritional values for 1 glass:

Carbohydrates 8.54g

Sugar 5.73g

Protein 8.78g

Total fat 2.04g

Sodium 69mg

Potassium 227mg

Calcium 117mg

Iron 2.79mg

Vitamins (Vitamin C total ascorbic acid; B-6; B-12; Folate-DFE; A-RAE; A-IU; D; D-D2+D3; K-phylloquinone; Thianin; Riboflavin; Niacin)

Calories 71.3

9. Apple and orange protein shake

Ingredients:

- 1 small apple
- 1 small orange
- ½ glass of water
- 1 tsp of brown sugar
- 1 tsp of honey
- 1 tsp of chopped almonds

Preparation:

Put all the ingredients in a blender for few minutes. Drink cold.

Nutritional values for 1 glass:

Carbohydrates 12.31g

Sugar 8.73g

Protein 6.98g

Total fat 3.09g

Sodium 81mg

Potassium 265.9mg

Calcium 109mg

Iron 1.54mg

Vitamins (Vitamin C total ascorbic acid; B-6; B-12; Folate-DFE; A-RAE; A-IU; E-alpha-tocopherol; D; D-D2+D3; K-phylloquinone; Thianin; Riboflavin; Niacin)

Calories 73.1

10. Fruit shake

Ingredients:

1 cup of blueberries

1 banana

½ tsp of cinnamon

½ glass of skim milk

1 tbsp of agave syrup

Preparation:

Peel the banana and cut into small pieces. Combine agave syrup with skim milk and boil briefly. Allow it to cool for a while. Mix the ingredients in a blender for about 30 seconds. Sprinkle with cinnamon and serve cold.

Nutritional values for one glass:

Carbohydrates 11.12g

Sugar 9.34g

Protein 6.52g

Total fat 3.21g

Sodium 93mg

Potassium 208.31mg

Calcium 113mg

Iron 3.21mg

Vitamins (Vitamin C total ascorbic acid; B-6; B-12; Folate-DFE; A-RAE; A-IU; E-alpha-tocopherol; D; D-D2+D3; K-phylloquinone; Thianin; Riboflavin; Niacin)

Calories 79.9

11. Oatmeal protein shake

Ingredients:

½ cups of oatmeal

1 cup of skim milk

¼ cup of water

1 tsp of vanilla extract

½ banana

Preparation:

This recipes takes only few minutes to prepare and it is super tasty. All you want to do is combine the ingredients in a blender and mix until smooth mixture for about 30-40 seconds. Leave in the refrigerator for 30 minutes. You can sprinkle some cinnamon on top.

Nutritional values for 1 glass:

Carbohydrates 13.32g

Sugar 7.17g

Protein 6.91g

Total fat 3.99g

Sodium 92mg

Potassium 263.2mg

Calcium 119mg

Iron 2.92mg

Vitamins (Vitamin C total ascorbic acid; B-6; B-12; Folate-DFE; A-RAE; A-IU; D; D-D2+D3; K-phylloquinone; Thianin; Riboflavin)

Calories 89

12. Peppermint protein shake

Ingredients:

2 cups of skim milk

1 tsp of cocoa powder

1 tsp of grated almonds

1 tbsp of fat free cream

½ tsp of peppermint extract

Preparation:

Boil the milk on a low temperature. Add peppermint extract and cocoa powder. Stir well for 2-3 minutes. Remove from the heath and allow it to cool for about 30 minutes. Now mix with the grated almonds and fat free cream and put in a blender for about 30 seconds.

Nutritional values for 1 glass:

Carbohydrates 10.32g

Sugar 7.34g

Protein 6.81g

Total fat 3.08g

Sodium 85.9mg

Potassium 243.3mg

Calcium 121mg

Iron 1.09mg

Vitamins (Vitamin C total ascorbic acid; B-6; B-12; Folate-DFE; A-RAE; A-IU; E-alpha-tocopherol; D; D-D2+D3; K-phylloquinone; Thianin; Riboflavin; Niacin)

Calories 68.2

13. Flaxseed oil protein shake

Ingredients:

½ cup of water

½ cup of skim milk

1 tbsp of grated walnuts

1 tbsp of goji berries

1 tbsp of flaxseed oil

1 tsp of vanilla extract

1 tbsp of brown sugar

Preparation:

Mix the ingredients in a blender for about 40 seconds, or until smooth mixture. Keep in the refrigerator and serve cold.

Nutritional values for 1 glass:

Carbohydrates 14.31g

Sugar 9.19g

Protein 7.81g

Total fat 3.09g

Sodium 83mg

Potassium 279.9mg

Calcium 129mg

Iron 3.09mg

Vitamins (Vitamin C total ascorbic acid; B-6; B-12; Folate-DFE; A-RAE; A-IU; E-alpha-tocopherol; D; D-D2+D3; K-phylloquinone; Thianin; Riboflavin; Niacin)

Calories 113

14. Cinnamon protein shake

Ingredients:

1 glass of skim milk

1 tsp of cocoa powder

1 tbsp of raisins

1 tbsp of pumpkin seeds

¼ tsp of cinnamon

Preparation:

Mix in a blender until smooth mixture. Serve with ice cubes. You can sprinkle some more cinnamon on top before serving.

Nutritional values for 1 glass:

Carbohydrates 12.9g

Sugar 9.27g

Protein 7.75g

Total fat 4.57g

Sodium 92.3mg

Potassium 262.7mg

Calcium 123.5mg

Iron 5.21mg

Vitamins (Vitamin C total ascorbic acid; B-6; B-12; Folate-DFE; A-RAE; A-IU; E-alpha-tocopherol; D; D-D2+D3; K-phylloquinone; Thianin; Riboflavin; Niacin)

Calories 86.7

15. Almond protein shake

Ingredients:

1 cup of skim milk

½ cup of water

2 egg whites

1 tbsp of grated almonds

1 tbsp of honey

½ cup of oatmeal

Preparation:

Separate the egg whites from the yolks. Combine with other ingredients and mix in a blender for 30-40 seconds. Allow it to cool in the refrigerator. Serve cold.

Nutritional values for 1 glass:

Carbohydrates 14.31g

Sugar 9.19g

Protein 7.91g

Total fat 4.54g

Sodium 103mg

Potassium 287.9mg

Calcium 122mg

Iron 4.29mg

Vitamins (Vitamin C; B-6; B-12; Folate-DFE; A-RAE; A-IU; E-alpha-tocopherol; D; D-D2+D3; K; Thianin; Riboflavin; Niacin)

Calories 91

16. Banana protein shake

Ingredients:

1 large banana

1 cup of skim milk

½ cup of water

1 tsp of vanilla extract

1 tbsp of agave syrup

Preparation:

Peel and chop banana into small cubes. Combine with other ingredients in a blender and mix for 30 seconds, until smooth mixture. Keep in the refrigerator and serve cold.

Nutritional values for 1 glass:

Carbohydrates 10.11g

Sugar 7.17g

Protein 8.91g

Total fat 3.23g

Sodium 95mg

Potassium 612.9mg

Calcium 119mg

Iron 2.88mg

Vitamins (Vitamin C total ascorbic acid; B-6; B-12; Folate-DFE; A-RAE; A-IU; E-alpha-tocopherol; D; D-D2+D3; K-phylloquinone; Thianin; Riboflavin; Niacin)

Calories 88

17. Bran flakes protein shake

Ingredients:

1 cup of skim milk

½ cup of water

½ cup of bran flakes

1 tbsp of brown sugar

1 tbsp of honey

1 tsp of cocoa

Preparation:

Mix in a blender for 30-40 seconds, or until smooth mixture. You can add some cinnamon, but this is optional. Allow it to cool in the refrigerator for about an hour. Serve cold.

Nutritional values for 1 glass:

Carbohydrates 11.7g

Sugar 10.01g

Protein 5.32g

Total fat 3.65g

Sodium 86.5mg

Potassium 262mg

Calcium 111mg

Iron 3.75mg

Vitamins (Vitamin C total ascorbic acid; B-6; B-12; Folate-DFE; A-RAE; A-IU; E;D; D-D2+D3; K-phylloquinone; Thianin; Riboflavin)

Calories 78.7

18. Wild berries protein shake

Ingredients:

½ cup of wild berries

½ cup of fresh wild berries juice

½ cup of water

1 tsp of blackberry extract

2 egg whites

1 handful of ice

Preparation:

Separate the egg whites from the yolks. Combine with other ingredients and mix in a blender for about 30 seconds. Serve cold.

Nutritional values for 1 glass:

Carbohydrates 13.01g

Sugar 9g

Protein 7.8g

Total fat 1.95g

Sodium 98mg

Potassium 234.7mg

Calcium 110mg

Iron 3.04mg

Vitamins (Vitamin C total ascorbic acid; B-6; B-12; Folate-DFE; A-RAE; A-IU; E-alpha-tocopherol; D; D-D2+D3; K-phylloquinone; Thianin; Riboflavin; Niacin)

Calories 68

19. Walnuts protein shake

Ingredients:

1 cup of coconut milk

½ cup of grated walnuts

½ cup of finely chopped spinach

1 whole egg

2 tbsp of brown sugar

1 tsp of walnut extract

Preparation:

Combine the ingredients in a blender and mix for 30-40 seconds. Add some ice cubes before serving.

Nutritional values for 1 glass:

Carbohydrates 11.27g

Sugar 8.11g

Protein 5.85g

Total fat 2.94g

Sodium 85mg

Potassium 259.6mg

Calcium 113mg

Iron 2.03mg

Vitamins (Vitamin C total ascorbic acid; B-6; B-12; Folate-DFE; A-RAE; A-IU; E-alpha-tocopherol; D; D-D2+D3; K-phylloquinone; Thianin; Riboflavin; Niacin)

Calories 72.6

20. Greek yogurt protein shake

Ingredients:

1 cup of Greek yogurt

1 tbsp of honey

1 tbsp of brown sugar

¼ cup of skim milk

1 tsp of almond butter

¼ tsp of cinnamon

Preparation:

Combine the milk, almond butter and brown sugar in a saucepan. Stir well and allow it to boil, on a low temperature for about 2 minutes. Remove from the heath and cool for 15 minutes. Pour the mixture in a blender and add other ingredients. Mix well for 30-40 seconds and keep in the refrigerator to cool.

Nutritional values for 1 glass:

Carbohydrates 13.1g

Sugar 9g

Protein 7.91g

Total fat 3.03g

Sodium 95mg

Potassium 259mg

Calcium 119mg

Iron 3mg

Vitamins (Vitamin C total ascorbic acid; B-6; B-12; Folate-DFE; A-RAE; A-IU; E-alpha-tocopherol; D; D-D2+D3; K-phylloquinone; Thianin; Riboflavin; Niacin)

Calories 70

21. Protein shake with eggs

Ingredients:

1 cup of skim milk

½ cup of water

1 tbsp of Greek yogurt

3 eggs

1 tsp of vanilla extract

1 tbsp of brown sugar

Preparation:

Combine the ingredients in a blender and mix until smooth mixture. Serve cold.

Nutritional values for 1 glass:

Carbohydrates 10g

Sugar 6.02g

Protein 9.84g

Total fat 3.94g

Sodium 95mg

Potassium 212.2mg

Calcium 123mg

Iron 2.43mg

Vitamins (Vitamin C;B-6; B-12; Folate-DFE; A-RAE; A-IU; D; D-D2+D3; K-phylloquinone; Thianin; Riboflavin; Niacin)

Calories 72

22. Peanut butter protein shake

Ingredients:

1 cup of skim milk

¼ cup of finely chopped peanuts

1 tbsp of peanut butter

1 tbsp of brown sugar

1 tbsp of goji berries

1 small green apple

Preparation:

Peel and chop the apple into thin slices. Use a saucepan to melt the peanut butter on a low temperature. Add brown sugar and stir well for 30 seconds. Remove from the heath and allow it to cool. Meanwhile, mix the other ingredients in a blender, add peanut and sugar and mix well for 30-40 seconds. Keep in the refrigerator for at least 30 minutes to cool.

Nutritional values for 1 glass:

Carbohydrates 13.2g

Sugar 10.7g

Protein 11.6g

Total fat 2.8g

Sodium 97mg

Potassium 259mg

Calcium 134.3mg

Iron 3.09mg

Vitamins (Vitamin C total ascorbic acid; B-6; B-12; Folate-DFE; A-RAE; A-IU; E-alpha-tocopherol; D; D-D2+D3; K-phylloquinone; Thianin; Riboflavin; Niacin)

Calories 88.4

23. Energy protein shake

Ingredients:

1 tbsp of grated almonds

1 tbsp of grated walnuts

1 tbsp of grated macadamian nuts

1 cup of aronia

1 medium banana

1 glass of fresh orange juice

1 glass of water

2 egg whites

2 tbsp of honey

1 tbsp of brown sugar

Preparation:

This protein shake is very easy to prepare. Simply combine the ingredients in a blender and mix well for 40 seconds. Cool well before serving.

Nutritional values for 1 glass:

Carbohydrates 17.47g

Sugar 14.03g

Protein 15.8g

Total fat 7.94g

Sodium 175mg

Potassium 369mg

Calcium 189mg

Iron 6.09mg

Vitamins (Vitamin C total ascorbic acid; B-6; B-12; Folate-DFE; A-RAE; A-IU; E-alpha-tocopherol; D; D-D2+D3; K-phylloquinone; Thianin; Riboflavin; Niacin)

Calories 149

24. Pistachio protein shake

Ingredients:

1 cup of skim milk

¼ cup of finely chopped pistachios

1 tbsp of peanut butter

1 tbsp of honey

1 handful of ice

Preparation:

Mix the ingredients in a blender until smooth mixture.

Nutritional values for 1 glass:

Carbohydrates 13.4g

Sugar 9.15g

Protein 7.81g

Total fat 5.91g

Sodium 105mg

Potassium 287mg

Calcium 115mg

Iron 3.03mg

Vitamins (Vitamin C total ascorbic acid; B-6; B-12; Folate-DFE; A-RAE; A-IU; E-alpha-tocopherol; D; D-D2+D3; K-phylloquinone; Thianin; Riboflavin; Niacin)

Calories 81

25. Almond butter protein shake

Ingredients:

1 cup of skim milk

½ cup of water

½ cup of oatmeal

1 tbsp of brown sugar

2 tbsp of almond butter

1 tsp of almond extract

¼ cup of almond milk

Preparation:

Boil the almond milk on a low temperature. Add almond extract, almond butter and brown sugar. Stir well and allow it to boil for 30-40 seconds. Remove from the heath and cool. Combine with other ingredients in a blender and mix well for 30 seconds. Serve cold.

Nutritional values for 1 glass:

Carbohydrates 15.3g

Sugar 8.11g

Protein 9.83g

Total fat 7.81g

Sodium 106mg

Potassium 297.2mg

Calcium 125mg

Iron 4.09mg

Vitamins (Vitamin C total ascorbic acid; B-6; B-12; Folate-DFE; A-RAE; A-IU; E-alpha-tocopherol; D; D-D2+D3; K-phylloquinone; Thianin; Riboflavin; Niacin)

Calories 73

26. Green apples protein shake

Ingredients:

1 green apple

2 egg whites

1 glass of fresh apple juice

1 tbsp of grated walnuts

¼ tsp of cinnamon

Preparation:

Peel and cut the apple into thin slices. Separate egg whites from the yolks. Mix with other ingredients in a blender for 30-40 seconds. Serve with ice cubes.

Nutritional values for 1 glass:

Carbohydrates 11g

Sugar 8g

Protein 8.92g

Total fat 3.44g

Sodium 92mg

Potassium 212.4mg

Calcium 103mg

Iron 3.03mg

Vitamins (Vitamin C total ascorbic acid; B-6; B-12; Folate-DFE; A-RAE; A-IU; E-alpha-tocopherol; D; D-D2+D3; K-phylloquinone; Thianin; Riboflavin; Niacin)

Calories 62

27. Honey and banana protein shake

Ingredients:

1 cup of skim milk

1 medium banana

1 tbsp of honey

1 tsp of banana extract

1 tbsp of Greek yogurt

1 tbsp of non fat cream

Preparation:

Peel and chop banana into small cubes. Mix with other ingredients in a blender for 30-40 seconds and allow it to cool in the refrigerator for about an hour. Serve cold.

Nutritional values for 1 glass:

Carbohydrates 12.7g

Sugar 7.1g

Protein 9.92g

Total fat 2.94g

Sodium 85mg

Potassium 249.5mg

Calcium 133mg

Iron 3mg

Vitamins (Vitamin C total ascorbic acid; B-6; B-12; Folate-DFE; A-RAE; A-IU; E-alpha-tocopherol; D; D-D2+D3; K-phylloquinone; Thianin; Riboflavin; Niacin)

Calories 68.9

28. Mixed nuts protein shake

Ingredients:

1 tsp of grated almonds

1 tsp of grated walnuts

1 tsp of grated hazelnuts

1 tsp of grated macadamian nuts

1 glass of fresh orange juice

1 tbsp of agave syrup

1 tbsp of non fat orange ice cream

1 handful of ice cubes

Preparation:

Mix the ingredients in a blender for 30-40 seconds.

Nutritional values for 1 glass:

Carbohydrates 15.19g

Sugar 11.23g

Protein 9.85g

Total fat 6.64g

Sodium 115mg

Potassium 309.6mg

Calcium 121mg

Iron 5.03mg

Vitamins (Vitamin C total ascorbic acid; B-6; B-12; Folate-DFE; A-RAE; A-IU; E-alpha-tocopherol; D; D-D2+D3; K-phylloquinone; Thianin; Riboflavin; Niacin)

Calories 98.3

29. Pineapple protein shake

Ingredients:

1 cup of chopped fresh pineapple

1 cup of fresh pineapple juice

2 egg whites

1 tbsp of brown sugar

1 tsp of pineapple extract

2 cherries for decoration

Preparation:

Separate the egg whites from the yolk. Mix with other ingredients in a blender for 30-40 seconds. Serve with ice and cherries on top.

Nutritional values for 1 glass:

Carbohydrates 11.34g

Sugar 8.11g

Protein 6.85g

Total fat 1.84g

Sodium 84mg

Potassium 209.6mg

Calcium 103mg

Iron 1.93mg

Vitamins (Vitamin C total ascorbic acid; B-6; B-12; Folate-DFE; A-RAE; A-IU; E-alpha-tocopherol; D; D-D2+D3; K-phylloquinone; Thianin; Riboflavin; Niacin)

Calories 58.9

30. Exotic protein shake

Ingredients:

1 cup of coconut milk

½ banana

½ cup of chopped pineapple

1 tsp of coconut extract

2 tbsp of low-fat sour cream

2 tbsp of brown sugar

Preparation:

Combine the ingredients in a blender for 30-40 seconds and mix well until smooth mixture. Serve with some ice cubes.

Nutritional values for 1 glass:

Carbohydrates 11.17g

Sugar 8.31g

Protein 5.85g

Total fat 2.44g

Sodium 82mg

Potassium 279.6mg

Calcium 114mg

Iron 2.3mg

Vitamins (Vitamin C total ascorbic acid; B-6; B-12; Folate-DFE; A-RAE; A-IU; E-alpha-tocopherol; D; D-D2+D3; K-phylloquinone; Thianin; Riboflavin; Niacin)

Calories 72

31. Peach and cream protein shake

Ingredients:

1 medium peach

1 glass of almond milk

1 tbsp of low-fat sour cream

1 tbsp of Greek yogurt

1 tsp of peach extract

1 tbsp of honey

1 tsp of pumpkin seeds

1 handful of ice

Preparation:

Cut the peach into small pieces. Mix with other ingredients in a blender until smooth mixture.

Nutritional values for 1 glass:

Carbohydrates 13.27g

Sugar 9.11g

Protein 7.85g

Total fat 4.94g

Sodium 85mg

Potassium 259mg

Calcium 103mg

Iron 2.93mg

Vitamins (Vitamin C total ascorbic acid; B-6; B-12; Folate-DFE; A-RAE; A-IU; E-alpha-tocopherol; D; D-D2+D3; K-phylloquinone; Thianin; Riboflavin; Niacin)

Calories 70

32. Greek vanilla yogurt protein shake

Ingredients:

1 cup of Greek vanilla yogurt

1 cup of skim milk

1 tbsp of grated macadamian nuts

1 medium banana

½ cup of strawberries

1 tsp of vanilla extract

Preparation:

Peel the banana and cut into small cubes. Combine with the other ingredients in a blender and mix until smooth mixture, about 30-40 seconds. You can sprinkle some vanilla powder on top, but this is optional. Serve cold.

Nutritional values for 1 glass:

Carbohydrates 12.2g

Sugar 6.1g

Protein 9.85g

Total fat 3.4g

Sodium 79mg

Potassium 216.6mg

Calcium 111mg

Iron 2.3mg

Vitamins (Vitamin C total ascorbic acid; B-6; B-12; Folate-DFE; A-RAE; A-IU; E-alpha-tocopherol; D; D-D2+D3; K-phylloquinone; Thianin; Riboflavin; Niacin)

Calories 78

33. Plum power shake

Ingredients:

3 ripe plums, pitted

1 cup of skim milk

½ cup of walnuts

¼ cup of agave syrup

Preparation:

Mix the ingredients in a blender for 30-40 seconds. Serve cold.

Nutritional values for 1 glass:

Carbohydrates 12.21g

Sugar 5.98g

Protein 6.23g

Total fat 2.31g

Sodium 82.5mg

Potassium 217.8mg

Calcium 124.3mg

Iron 1.27mg

Vitamins (Vitamin C total ascorbic acid; B-6; B-12; Folate-DFE; A-RAE; A-IU; E-alpha-tocopherol; D; D-D2+D3; K-phylloquinone; Thianin; Riboflavin; Niacin)

Calories 56.4

34. Lemon protein shake

Ingredients:

1 glass of fresh lemonade, without sugar

1 tbsp of lemon zest

2 tbsp of brown sugar

½ cup of cottage cheese

1 tbsp of vanilla extract

1 tbsp of grated oat crackers

Preparation:

Put the ingredients into a blender and blend until you get a creamy consistency. Pour it in a glass and sprinkle with grated oat crackers. Serve cold.

Nutritional values for 1 glass:

Carbohydrates 9.27g

Sugar 6.11g

Protein 8.85g

Total fat 4.94g

Sodium 86mg

Potassium 211.4mg

Calcium 115mg

Iron 1.05mg

Vitamins (Vitamin C total ascorbic acid; B-6; B-12; Folate-DFE; A-RAE; A-IU; E-alpha-tocopherol; D; D-D2+D3; K-phylloquinone; Thianin; Riboflavin; Niacin)

Calories 57.6

35. Caramel protein shake

Ingredients:

1 cup of skim milk

½ cup of brown sugar

½ tsp of cinnamon

1 tsp of chocolate extract

1 tbsp of grated almonds

1 medium pear, chopped into small pieces

2 tbsp of Greek yogurt

Preparation:

Use a saucepan to melt the sugar on a low temperature. Slowly add the milk and stir well for about a minute. Your sugar will become a nice caramel. Remove from the heath and allow it to cool for a while. Meanwhile cut a pear into small pieces, combine with other ingredients in a blender, add caramel and blend for about 40 seconds. Pour the protein shake into a glass, sprinkle with cinnamon and add some ice cubes.

Nutritional values for 1 glass:

Carbohydrates 12.37g

Sugar 8.42g

Protein 6.85g

Total fat 2.74g

Sodium 83mg

Potassium 239.6mg

Calcium 112mg

Iron 2.05mg

Vitamins (Vitamin C total ascorbic acid; B-6; B-12; Folate-DFE; A-RAE; A-IU; E-alpha-tocopherol; D; D-D2+D3; K-phylloquinone; Thianin; Riboflavin; Niacin)

Calories 72.7

36. Hazelnuts protein shake

Ingredients:

1 cup of skim milk

½ cup of chocolate Greek yogurt

1 tsp of cocoa powder

2 tbsp of grated hazelnuts

1 tbsp of brown sugar

2 egg whites

Preparation:

Combine the ingredients in a blender and mix until creamy mixture. Allow it to cool in the refrigerator for about 30 minutes.

Nutritional values for 1 glass:

Carbohydrates 11.27g

Sugar 8.13g

Protein 9.84g

Total fat 2.94g

Sodium 82mg

Potassium 253.6mg

Calcium 112mg

Iron 2.08mg

Vitamins (Vitamin C total ascorbic acid; B-6; B-12; Folate-DFE; A-RAE; A-IU; E-alpha-tocopherol; D; D-D2+D3; K-phylloquinone; Thianin; Riboflavin; Niacin)

Calories 62.6

37. Chocolate and coffee protein shake

Ingredients:

1 cup of strong black coffee, without sugar

½ cup of low-fat cream

3 tbsp of Greek yogurt

1 tbsp of brown sugar

1 tsp of cocoa

¼ cup of grated dark chocolate (80% of cocoa)

1 tbsp of grated hazelnuts

Preparation:

Mix the ingredients in a blender for 30-40 seconds. Keep in the refrigerator and serve with ice cubes. Sprinkle some grated hazelnuts on top.

Nutritional values for 1 glass:

Carbohydrates 15.27g

Sugar 8.51g

Protein 10.83g

Total fat 6.94g

Sodium 83mg

Potassium 259.3mg

Calcium 143mg

Iron 2.23mg

Vitamins (Vitamin C total ascorbic acid; B-6; B-12; Folate-DFE; A-RAE; A-IU; E-alpha-tocopherol; D; D-D2+D3; K-phylloquinone; Thianin; Riboflavin; Niacin)

Calories 74

38. Cherry protein shake

Ingredients:

1 cup of fresh cherry juice, without sugar

1 cup of cherries

½ cup of Greek yogurt

1 tsp of cherry extract

1 tbsp of brown sugar

1 handful of ice

Preparation:

You just need to mix the ingredients in a blender for 30 seconds. Serve cold.

Nutritional values for 1 glass:

Carbohydrates 10.67g

Sugar 8.11g

Protein 8.65g

Total fat 2.54g

Sodium 95mg

Potassium 159.6mg

Calcium 93mg

Iron 1.03mg

Vitamins (Vitamin C total ascorbic acid; B-6; B-12; A-RAE; A-IU; E-alpha-tocopherol; D; K-phylloquinone; Thianin; Riboflavin; Niacin)

Calories 74.6

39. Mango protein shake

Ingredients:

1 cup of chopped mango

½ cup of oatmeal

1 tsp of pumpkin seeds

1 tsp of almond butter

1 cup of skim milk

1 tbsp of low-fat cream

2 tbsp of brown sugar

Preparation:

Combine the ingredients and blend until incorporated. Top with some mango extract powder, but this is optional. Serve cold.

Nutritional values for 1 glass:

Carbohydrates 14.24g

Sugar 8.11g

Protein 10.85g

Total fat 6.94g

Sodium 75mg

Potassium 249.6mg

Calcium 103mg

Iron 2.93mg

Vitamins (Vitamin C total ascorbic acid; B-6; B-12; Folate-DFE; A-RAE; A-IU; E-alpha-tocopherol; D; D-D2+D3; K-phylloquinone; Thianin; Riboflavin; Niacin)

Calories 82.6

40. Forest pleasure protein shake

Ingredients:

1 cup of fresh apple juice

½ cup of water

½ medium green apple

½ medium carrot

½ small peach

½ cup of mixed forest berries (raspberries, strawberries,blackberries)

½ cup of cottage cheese

1 tbsp of agave syrup

Preparation:

Mix in a blender until smooth mixture. Allow it to cool in the refrigerator for a while.

Nutritional values for 1 glass:

Carbohydrates 11.27g

Sugar 8.41g

Protein 9.85g

Total fat 4.94g

Sodium 84mg

Potassium 159.6mg

Calcium 84mg

Iron 1.3mg

Vitamins (Vitamin C total ascorbic acid; B-6; B-12; Folate-DFE; A-RAE; A-IU; E-alpha-tocopherol; D; D-D2+D3; K-phylloquinone; Thianin; Riboflavin; Niacin)

Calories 59

41. Ginger protein shake

Ingredients:

1 medium banana

1 cup of low-fat yogurt

1 cup of finely chopped spinach

1 tsp of grated ginger

2 egg whites

1 tsp of lemon juice

2 tbsp of honey

Preparation:

Separate egg whites from yolks. Mix with other ingredients in a blender for about 30 seconds, until foamy mixture.

Nutritional values for 1 glass:

Carbohydrates 10g

Sugar 5.11g

Protein 9.85g

Total fat 4.94g

Sodium 83mg

Potassium 229.6mg

Calcium 115mg

Iron 2.13mg

Vitamins (Vitamin C total ascorbic acid; B-6; B-12; Folate-DFE; A-RAE; A-IU; E-alpha-tocopherol; D; D-D2+D3; K-phylloquinone; Thianin; Riboflavin; Niacin)

Calories 74.6

42. Papaya protein shake

Ingredients:

1 cup of papaya puree

½ cup of oatmeal

1 cup of skim milk

½ cup of water

1 tbsp of goji berries

1 tbsp of agave syrup

2 tbsp of brown sugar

Preparation:

Combine the ingredients in a blender and mix well until smooth mixture. Serve with some ice cubes.

Nutritional values for 1 glass:

Carbohydrates 11.2g

Sugar 7.11g

Protein 9.85g

Total fat 2.44g

Sodium 84mg

Potassium 178.6mg

Calcium 113mg

Iron 2.03mg

Vitamins (Vitamin C total ascorbic acid; B-6; B-12; Folate-DFE; A-RAE; A-IU; E-alpha-tocopherol; D; D-D2+D3; K-phylloquinone; Thianin; Riboflavin; Niacin)

Calories 69.5

43. Blueberries protein shake

Ingredients:

1 cup of skim milk

1 cup of blueberries

1 tbsp of brown sugar

1 tsp of mint extract

Preparation:

Very simple to prepare. This protein is very refreshing and it only takes about 2-3 minutes to prepare it. Just mix the ingredients in a blender for 30 seconds and serve with ice cubes.

Nutritional values for 1 glass:

Carbohydrates 7g

Sugar 3.11g

Protein 5.8g

Total fat 1.94g

Sodium 65mg

Potassium 159.3mg

Calcium 87mg

Iron 1.03mg

Vitamins (Vitamin C total ascorbic acid; B-6; B-12; Folate-DFE; A-RAE; A-IU; E-alpha-tocopherol; D; D-D2+D3; K-phylloquinone; Thianin; Riboflavin; Niacin)

Calories 54

44. Pumpkin pie protein shake

Ingredients:

1 cup of pumpkin puree

1 cup of skim milk

1 tbsp of brown sugar

2 egg whites

1 medium banana

1 small green apple

1 tsp of cinnamon

Preparation:

Separate the egg whites from yolks. Peel and grate the apple. Cut banana into small pieces and combine the ingredients in a blender for 30-40 seconds. Sprinkle some cinnamon on top and leave in the refrigerator to cool for a while.

Nutritional values for 1 glass:

Carbohydrates 11.36g

Sugar 8.03g

Protein 10.23g

Total fat 3.87g

Sodium 79.43mg

Potassium 208.1mg

Calcium 104.9mg

Iron 1.89mg

Vitamins (Vitamin C total ascorbic acid; B-6; B-12; Folate-DFE; A-RAE; A-IU; E-alpha-tocopherol; D; D-D2+D3; K-phylloquinone; Thianin; Riboflavin; Niacin)

Calories 72.7

45. Raspberries and cream protein shake

Ingredients:

1 cup of frozen raspberries

½ cup of low-fat cream

½ cup of low-fat raspberries ice cream

1 cup of water

1 tbsp of honey

Preparation:

Mix the ingredients in a blender for 30-40 seconds. Drink cold.

Nutritional values for 1 glass:

Carbohydrates 11.27g

Sugar 8.31g

Protein 5.85g

Total fat 2.24g

Sodium 86mg

Potassium 239.6mg

Calcium 112mg

Iron 2.55mg

Vitamins (Vitamin C;B-6; B-12; Folate-DFE; A-RAE; A-IU; E-alpha-tocopherol; D; D-D2+D3; Niacin)

Calories 72.6

Carbohydrates 13.67g

Sugar 9.11g

Protein 9.85g

Total fat 4.94g

Sodium 89mg

Potassium 261.6mg

Calcium 119mg

Iron 2.93mg

Vitamins (Vitamin C total ascorbic acid; B-6; B-12; Folate-DFE; A-RAE; A-IU; E-alpha-tocopherol; D; D-D2+D3; K-phylloquinone; Thianin; Riboflavin; Niacin)

Calories 75.9

PRE-COMPETITION MUSCLE MEALS FOR BODYBUILDING

1. Boiled eggs with chopped basil

Ingredients:

2 eggs

1 tsp of chopped basil

pepper

Preparation:

Boil eggs for 10 minutes. Peel and chop into small pieces. Sprinkle with chopped basil.

Nutritional values per 100 g:

Carbohydrates 1.1g

Sugar 0g

Protein 13g

Total fat (good monounsaturated fat) 11g

Sodium 124mg

Potassium 126mg

Calcium 50mg

Iron 1.2mg

Vitamins (vitamin A; B-6; B-12; C)

Calories 155

2. Beef sirloin with slices of eggplant

Ingredients:

1 thin beef sirloin

1 medium eggplant

1 tsp of olive oil

chopped basil

pepper

Preparation:

Wash and pepper the meat. Grill it on a barbecue pan for about 10 minutes on each side. Remove from pan. Peel eggplant and cut two thick slices. Fry for few minutes in the same barbecue pan. Remove from heat and serve with beef. Sprinkle with chopped basil.

Nutritional values:

Carbohydrates 6g

Sugar 1.2g

Protein 35.2 g

Total fat 4.9g

Sodium 57 mg

Potassium 397mg

Calcium 18.5mg

Iron 1.9mg

Vitamins (vitamin A; B-6; B-12; C; D; D2; D3; K;Thiamin; K)

Calories 212

3. Tomato and walnuts salad

Ingredients:

1 big tomato

½ cup of chopped walnuts

1 tsp of lemon juice

Preparation:

Wash and cut tomato into small pieces. Add chopped walnuts and mix well. Pour lemon juice over it.

Nutritional values for 1 cup:

Carbohydrates 8.2g

Sugar 3.8g

Protein 10g

Total fat 4.5g

Sodium 17 mg

Potassium 112mg

Calcium 16.5mg

Iron 1.3mg

Vitamins (vitamin A; B-6; B-12; C; D; D2; D3; K; Riboflavin; Niacin; Thiamin; K)

Calories 218

4. Cooked chard with olive oil

Ingredients:

1 bunch of chard

1 tsp of olive oil

1 tsp of tumeric

Preparation:

Wash and chop chard. Fry it in olive oil for 20 minutes on a low temperature, or until tender. Add tumeric before serving.

Nutritional values for one cup:

Carbohydrates 6.9g

Sugar 2.1g

Protein 8.4 g

Total fat 1.9g

Sodium 34.2 mg

Potassium 23.2mg

Calcium 12.4mg

Iron 0.59mg

Vitamins (vitamin A; B-6; B-12; C; D; D2; D3; K; Riboflavin; Niacin; Thiamin; K)

Calories 113

5. Baked mushrooms with rosemary

Ingredients:

1 cup of mushrooms

1 tsp of olive oil

1 tsp of chopped rosemary

Preparation:

Bake mushrooms in a barbecue pan for 5-7 minutes. Remove from pan and sprinkle with olive oil and chopped rosemary.

Nutritional values for one cup:

Carbohydrates 6.2g

Sugar 1.1g

Protein 8.4 g

Total fat (good monounsaturated fat) 1.3g

Sodium 48.2 mg

Potassium 23.2mg

Calcium 12.4mg

Iron 0.59mg

Vitamins (vitamin A; B-6; B-12; C; D; D2; D3; K; Riboflavin; Niacin; Thiamin; K)

Calories 117

6. Octopus salad with tomatoes and capers

Ingredients:

1 cup of frozen cut octopus

¼ cup of capers

½ cup of olives

5 cherry tomatoes

1 tsp of chopped parsley

1 tsp of chopped celery

1 small onion

2 cloves of garlic

1 tsp of chopped rosemary

1 tbsp of olive oil

1 tsp of lemon juice

Preparation:

Cook the octopus in salted water until tender. It usually takes about 20-30 minutes. Remove from pot, wash and drain. Wash and cut vegetables and mix with octopus. Mix the spices and add to salad. Sprinkle with olive oil and lemon juice. Cool well before serving.

Nutritional values for one cup:

Carbohydrates 12.9g

Sugar 5.1g

Protein 16.4 g

Total fat (good monounsaturated fat) 9.9g

Sodium 114.2 mg

Potassium 83.2mg

Calcium 42.4mg

Iron 0.59mg

Vitamins (vitamin A; B-6; B-12; C; D; D2; D3; K; Riboflavin; Niacin; Thiamin; K)

Calories 81

7. Grilled zucchini with garlic and parsley

Ingredients:

1 medium zucchini

1 tbsp of chopped parsley

2 cloves of garlic

Preparation:

Peel the zucchini and cut into 4 slices. Fry in a barbecue pan for 3-4 minutes. Add chopped garlic and bake for another 5 minutes. Sprinkle with parsley before serving.

Nutritional values:

Carbohydrates 3.71g

Sugar 3g

Protein 2 g

Total fat 0g

Sodium 2.9 mg

Potassium 360mg

Calcium 0.2mg

Iron 0.3mg

Vitamins (vitamin A; B-6; B-12; C; D:K)

Calories 20

8. Mixed fruits and vegetables shake

Ingredients:

1 cup of mixed blueberries, raspberries, blackberries and strawberries

½ cup of chopped baby spinach

2 cups of water

Preparation:

Mix ingredients in a blender for few minutes.

Nutritional values for 1 cup:

Carbohydrates 9.2g

Sugar 6.15g

Protein 8.75g

Total fat 0.87g

Sodium 54.8mg

Potassium 107.8mg

Calcium 82mg

Iron 2.03mg

Vitamins (Vitamin C total ascorbic acid; B-6; B-12; Folate-DFE; A-RAE; A-IU; E-alpha-tocopherol; D; D-D2+D3; K-phylloquinone; Thianin; Riboflavin; Niacin)

Calories 42.6

9. Fish stew

Ingredients:

1 carp fillet

1 carrot

2 chili peppers

1 medium tomato

pepper

celery roots and leaf

Preparation:

It is the best to buy cooked carrots, or cook them before preparing the fish stew. Wash and cut vegetables, mix with celery and fish and put in a pot. Pour little water, just to cover it. Cook on a low temperature for 20-30 minutes.

Nutritional values:

Carbohydrates 8.2g

Sugar 3.9g

Protein 15.2 g

Total fat (good monounsaturated fat) 6.6g

Sodium 113.8 mg

Potassium 71mg

Calcium 29.1mg

Iron 0.32mg

Vitamins (vitamin A; B-6; B-12; C; D; D2; D3; K; Riboflavin; Niacin; Thiamin; K)

Calories 172

10. Pineapple omelet with almonds

Ingredients:

3 slices of pineapple

2 eggs

½ cup of almonds

1 tbsp of flaxseed oil for frying

Preparation:

Beat the eggs and add almonds. Fry pineapple slices for few minutes on both sides, without oil. When done, remove from pan, add oil, heat it and add eggs mixture. Serve with baked pineapple slices.

Nutritional values per 100g:

Carbohydrates 8.9g

Sugar 4.6g

Protein 19.2 g

Total fat 13.6g

Sodium 134.8 mg

Potassium 131mg

Calcium 67.1mg

Iron 1.52mg

Vitamins (vitamin A; B-12; C; K; Riboflavin; Niacin; K)

Calories 187

11. Beef chop with pineapple and tumeric

Ingredients:

1 medium beef chop

1 tbsp of olive oil

1 tsp of tumeric

Pepper

2 pineapple slices

Preparation:

Wash and dry the meat. Fry it without oil, in it's own sauce, for 15-20 minutes on low temperature. Remove from heat. Make a sauce with olive oil, tumeric and pepper and spread it over fried beef. Fry it once more for 3-4 minutes, add pineapple slices and serve warm.

Nutritional values per 100g:

Carbohydrates 15.7g

Sugar 9.9g

Protein 34g

Total fat (good monounsaturated fat) 17.6g

Sodium 99.3 mg

Potassium 328mg

Calcium 49.1mg

Iron 0.52mg

Vitamins (vitamin A; B-6; B-12; C; D; D2; D3; K; Riboflavin; Niacin; Thiamin; K)

Calories 311

12. Fruit salad

Ingredients:

1 cup of berries

½ cup of pineapple cubes

½ cup of chopped apple

1 tsp of cinnamon

1 tsp of agave syrup

Preparation:

Mix fruits, add agave syrup and sprinkle with cinnamon.

Nutritional values for one cup:

Carbohydrates 19.2g

Sugar 12g

Protein 15.2 g

Total fat (good monounsaturated fat) 4.6g

Sodium 123.8 mg

Potassium 95mg

Calcium 44.1mg

Iron 0.52mg

Vitamins (vitamin A; B-6; B-12; C; D; D2; D3; K; Riboflavin; Niacin; Thiamin; K)

Calories 77

13. Tuna salad with lettuce and curry

Ingredients:

1 small can of tuna without oil

1 bunch of lettuce

2 chili peppers

1 tsp of curry

1 tsp of lemon sauce

Preparation:

Wash and cut lettuce. Mix it with tuna, add chopped chili peppers and lemon sauce. Sprinkle with curry.

Nutritional values for 1 cup:

Carbohydrates 23.4g

Sugar 13g

Protein 33.2g

Total fat (good monounsaturated fat) 12.4g

Sodium 123mg

Potassium 72.3mg

Calcium 42.1mg

Iron 0.27mg

Vitamins (vitamin A; B-6; B-12; C; D; D2; D3; K; Riboflavin; Niacin; Thiamin; K)

Calories 68

14. Turkey drumstick with nutmeg and carob

Ingredients:

1 turkey drumstick

½ cup of water

½ cup of nutmeg

½ cup of carob

Preparation:

Wash and clean the meat. Fry it for about 15 minutes in it's own sauce (add some water while frying the turkey). Finely chop nutmeg and carob and add to saucepan. Mix well with turkey sauce. Remove from the pan and sprinkle with some more carob.

Nutritional values for one cup:

Carbohydrates 3.2g

Sugar 0.9g

Protein 31g

Total fat (good monounsaturated fat) 10.4g

Sodium 998mg

Potassium 78.2mg

Calcium 48mg

Iron 0.37mg

Vitamins (vitamin A; B-6; B-12; C; D; D2; D3; K; Riboflavin; Niacin; Thiamin; K)

Calories 210

15. Grilled eggplant slices with chopped fennel

Ingredients:

1 large eggplant

½ cup of chopped fennel

1 tbsp of olive oil

1 tsp of chopped parsley

Preparation:

Peel the eggplant and cut into 3 slices. Bake it in a barbecue pan without oil. When done, spread olive oil over it, sprinkle with fennel and parsley.

(These eggplant slices are great cold, so you can leave them overnight in a refrigerator)

Nutritional values per slice:

Carbohydrates 8.9g

Sugar 3g

Protein 7g

Total fat (good monounsaturated fat) 2.4g

Sodium 54mg

Potassium 32.5mg

Calcium 12.4mg

Iron 0.37mg

Vitamins (vitamin A; B-6; B-12; C; D; D2; D3; K; Riboflavin; Niacin; Thiamin; K)

Calories 54

16.Spinach omelet

Ingredients:

1 cup of chopped spinach

2 eggs

1 tbsp of olive oil for frying

Preparation:

Cook spinach in salted water until tender. Remove from pan and drain. Fry in olive oil for 5-6 minutes and add eggs. Mix well and serve warm.

Nutritional values per 100g:

Carbohydrates 1.9g

Sugar 0.6g

Protein 19.2 g

Total fat 13.6g

Sodium 144mg

Potassium 133mg

Calcium 71mg

Iron 1.8mg

Vitamins (vitamin A; B-12; C; K; Riboflavin; Niacin; K)

Calories 177

17.Eggplant casserole

Ingredients:

2 large eggplants

1 cup of minced meat

1 medium onion

1 tsp of olive oil

pepper

2 medium tomatoes

1 tsp of chopped parsley

Preparation:

Peel the eggplants and cut lengthwise into thin sheets. Put them in a bowl, and leave them to sit for at least an hour. Roll them in beaten eggs. Fry in hot oil. Cut the onion, fry, add sliced peppers, tomato, which is cut into cubes, and finely chopped parsley. Fry for few minutes and then add the meat. When meat is tender, remove from heat, cool, add 1 egg and season with pepper. Put fried eggplant and meat with vegetables in an ovenproof dish and make layers until you have used all the material. Bake for 30 minutes at 300 degrees.

Nutritional values per 100g:

Carbohydrates 7.9g

Sugar 3.4g

Protein 10.2 g

Total fat 13.6g

Sodium 164mg

Potassium 302mg

Calcium 21.1mg

Iron 1.32mg

Vitamins (vitamin A; B-12; C; K; Riboflavin; Niacin; K)

Calories 109

18. Leek with chicken cubes

Ingredients:

2 cups of trimmed leeks

1 cup of chicken fillets, cut into cubes

olive oil

thyme leaves for decoration

salt to taste

Preparation:

Cut the leeks into small pieces and wash it under cold water, day before serving. Leave it overnight in a plastic bag.

Heat the oil in a large pan. Add chicken cubes and fry for about 15 minutes on a medium temperature. Add leaks, mix well and fry for another 10 minutes on a low temperature. Remove from the saucepan and allow it to cool. Decorate with thyme leaves.

Nutritional values for 1 cup:

Carbohydrates 7g

Sugar 1.6g

Protein 18.1 g

Total fat 13.6g

Sodium 124.1 mg

Potassium 120mg

Calcium 69.3mg

Iron 1.42mg

Vitamins (vitamin A; B-6; B-12; C; D; D2; D3; K; Riboflavin; Niacin; Thiamin; K)

Calories 187

19. Cooked mushrooms with vegetables

Ingredients:

2 cups of button mushrooms

1cup of dried turkey cubes

2 large carrots

½ cup of chopped cabbage

1 tsp of ginger

1 tbsp of olive oil

1 tsp of chopped parsley

Preparation:

Cook vegetables in water until tender. Remove from pan and drain. Allow it to cool for a while. Mix olive oil, ginger and parsley, add little water and cook it for few minutes, on a medium heat. Pour over vegetables, add dried turkey and mix well. Allow it to cool in the refrigerator for about 30 minutes before serving.

Nutritional values for 1 cup:

Carbohydrates 18.6g

Sugar 11.3g

Protein 21.9g

Total fat 14.2g

Sodium 153.3 mg

Potassium 89.8mg

Calcium 49.9mg

Iron 0.42mg

Vitamins (vitamin A; B-6; B-12; C; D; D2; D3; K; Riboflavin; Niacin; Thiamin; K)

Calories 79

20. Chicken wings with tumeric sauce

Ingredients:

2 chicken wings

1 tsp of tumeric

1 tbsp of olive oil

½ tsp of dried rosemary

¼ tsp of red pepper

Preparation:

Fry chicken wings in a barbecue pan for 10-15 minutes. 3-4 minutes before chicken is done, add olive oil, tumeric, rosemary, pepper and a little water. Mix well the sauce and soak the chicken in it.

Nutritional values per 100g:

Carbohydrates 18.6g

Sugar 0.9g

Protein 28g

Total fat 22.7g

Sodium 431.3 mg

Potassium 189mg

Calcium 2.9mg

Iron 2.42mg

Vitamins (vitamin A; B-6; B-12; C; D; D2; D3; K; Riboflavin; Niacin; Thiamin; K)

Calories 318

21.Tomato and tuna salad

Ingredients:

2 large tomatoes

2 medium onions

3 cans of tuna

1 tbsp of olive oil

1 tsp of lemon juice

basil

salt to taste

Preparation:

Wash and peel the vegetables. Cut it into small cubes. Add olive oil, lemon juice and basil. Mix well.

Nutritional values for one cup:

Carbohydrates 17.9g

Sugar 9.1g

Protein 28.3 g

Total fat (good monounsaturated fat) 15.8g

Sodium 127mg

Potassium 89.6mg

Calcium 42.1mg

Iron 0.38mg

Vitamins (vitamin A; B-6; B-12; C; D; D2; D3; K; Riboflavin; Niacin; Thiamin; K)

Calories 99

22. Veal steak with red pepper sauce

Ingredients:

1 medium veal steak

1 large red paprika

1 tsp of red pepper

1 tbsp of olive oil

chopped rosemary

Preparation:

Wash and cut paprika into small pieces. Put in a large pan, add olive oil and rosemary. Stew for 15 minutes on low heat. Add red pepper and cook for another few minutes. Wash and dry the steak. Fry it in a barbecue pan until tender. Add sauce and remove from pan.

Nutritional values per 100g:

Carbohydrates 4.5g

Sugar 2.1g

Protein 26 g

Total fat 9.8g

Sodium 87 mg

Potassium 339mg

Calcium 2.1mg

Iron 0.16mg

Vitamins (vitamin A; B-6; B-12; C; D; D2; D3; K)

Calories 203

23.Mushroom omelet

Ingredients:

1 cup of mushrooms,

2 eggs

1 tbsp of olive oil

Preparation:

Fry the mushrooms in olive oil on a low temperature. Let the mushroom sauce evaporate. Add eggs and mix well.

Nutritional values per 100 g:

Carbohydrates 4.1g

Sugar 0g

Protein 18g

Total fat (good monounsaturated fat) 11g

Sodium 126mg

Potassium 124mg

Calcium 14.9mg

Iron 1.8mg

Vitamins (vitamin A; B-6; B-12; C)

Calories 174

24. Turkey fillet with walnuts and maple syrup

Ingredients:

3 turkey fillets

½ cup of walnuts

1 tsp of maple syrup

¼ cup of water

1 tbsp of olive oil

salt to taste

Preparation:

Fry the fillets in a barbecue pan on a low temperature for about 15 minutes, or until tender. Remove from the heath and add water, maple syrup and walnuts. Mix well and fry for another 5-6 minutes until the water evaporates. Allow it to cool for a while.

Nutritional values per 100 g:

Carbohydrates 10.1g

Sugar 7.3g

Protein 24.2g

Total fat 8.7g

Sodium 1025mg

Potassium 126mg

Calcium 50mg

Iron 1.2mg

Vitamins (vitamin A; B-6; C)

Calories 148

25. Roasted cherry tomatoes, eggplant and basil salad

Ingredients:

1 small eggplant

5 egg whites

1 cup of cherry tomatoes

1 tsp of fresh chopped basil

1 tbsp of olive oil

white pepper to taste

1 tsp of lemon juice

Preparation:

Cut eggplant into thick pieces, dice shape. Salt the eggplant cubes, add oil, egg whites and place on a baking sheet. If necessary, add some more olive oil (this is optional). Bake for about 10 minutes in preheated oven at 350 degrees. Clean the cherry tomatoes and fry for about 15 minutes on a low temperature, using a small saucepan. You want to get lightly caramelized tomato sauce. Remove from the heath and allow it to cool for a while. Gently stir in the lemon sauce, olive oil and fresh basil. Pour over the eggplant and serve cold. A great side dish with barbecue or grilled fish. You can keep it in the fridge up to one week.

Nutritional values per slice:

Carbohydrates 10.4g

Sugar 3g

Protein 19g

Total fat (good monounsaturated fat) 4.9g

Sodium 52mg

Potassium 38.3mg

Calcium 12.9mg

Iron 0.32mg

Vitamins (vitamin A; B-6; B-12; C; D; D2; D3; K; Riboflavin; Niacin; Thiamin; K)

Calories 87

26.Nutmeg omelet

Ingredients:

3 eggs

2 tbsp of olive oil

1 tsp of nutmeg

1/5 tsp of pepper

Preparation:

Beat the eggs and add nutmeg and pepper. Mix well and fry in olive oil for few minutes. Serve warm. You can add some salt if you like.

Nutritional values per 100g:

Carbohydrates 0.9g

Sugar 0.45g

Protein 12g

Total fat 12.4g

Sodium 156mg

Potassium 117.5mg

Calcium 4.4mg

Iron 7.37mg

Vitamins (vitamin A; B-6; D; D2; D3)

Calories 156

27.Shrimps in tomato sauce

Ingredients:

2 cups of frozen shrimps

1 large tomato

1 tsp of dried basil

2 cloves of garlic

3 tbsp of olive oil

salt to taste

Preparation:

Grill frozen shrimps in a barbecue pan without oil. Wash and cut tomato into small pieces, add chopped basil, chopped garlic and olive oil. Cook it for 5-6 minutes (add some water if necessary). Pour the sauce over the grilled shrimps. Serve with lettuce.

Nutritional values per 100g:

Carbohydrates 7.9g

Sugar 4.2g

Protein 28g

Total fat (good monounsaturated fat) 1.32g

Sodium 131mg

Potassium 269.5mg

Calcium 8.7mg

Iron 4.37mg

Vitamins (vitamin A; B-6; B-12; C; D; D2; D3; K; Riboflavin; Niacin; Thiamin; K)

Calories 164

28. Lettuce salad

Ingredients:

1 bunch of lettuce

1 tbsp of olive oil

1 tsp of lemon juice

Preparation:

Wash and cut the lettuce, add olive oil and lemon juice. It is the best to prepare this salad before serving a meal. Don't let it stand long.

Nutritional values per 1 cup:

Carbohydrates 1.2g

Sugar 0.3g

Protein 1.7g

Total fat (good monounsaturated fat) 1.4g

Sodium 19mg

Potassium 132mg

Calcium 1.4mg

Iron 2.3mg

Vitamins (vitamin A; B-6; B-12; C;K)

Calories 25

29. Coriander salad

Ingredients:

1 cup of chopped coriander

1 boiled egg

2 cups of cherry tomatoes

1 tsp of tumeric

2 tbsp of olive oil

1 tsp of lemon sauce

salt to taste

Preparation:

Wash and cut cherry tomatoes and mix with coriander. Add tumeric, olive oil and lemon sauce.

Nutritional values for one cup:

Carbohydrates 14.2g

Sugar 8.9g

Protein 10g

Total fat (good monounsaturated fat) 9.6g

Sodium 122.2 mg

Potassium 81mg

Calcium 45.5mg

Iron 0.37mg

Vitamins (vitamin A; B-6; B-12; C; D; D2; D3; K; Riboflavin; Niacin; Thiamin; K)

Calories 55

30.Fried eggs with chopped mint

Ingredients:

3 eggs

1 tbsp of olive oil

1 tbsp of chopped mint

1 cup of cherry tomatoes

1 small onion

pepper to taste

salt to taste

Preparation:

Cut the vegetables into small pieces and fry in large saucepan on a low temperature for about 15 minutes. Wait for the water to evaporate. Beat the eggs and add chopped mint. Mix with vegetables, add olive oil and fry for few minutes. Before serving add some salt and pepper to taste.

Nutritional values per 100 g:

Carbohydrates 8.1g

Sugar 4g

Protein 28g

Total fat (good monounsaturated fat) 11.9g

Sodium 176mg

Potassium 174mg

Calcium 17.9mg

Iron 1.5mg

Vitamins (vitamin A; B-6; B-12; C; D; D2; D3; K; Riboflavin; Niacin; Thiamin; K)

Calories 194

31. Veal chop with chopped cloves

Ingredients:

2 large veal chops

1 cup of chopped cloves

4 tbsp of olive oil

1 tbsp of dried parsley

1 tsp of rosemary

1 tsp of red pepper

1 tbsp of lemon juice

Preparation:

Mix well the cloves, olive oil, parsley and rosemary to get a nice sauce. Wash the steak and put it in a small baking tray. Add sauce and bake for 15-20 minutes at 300 degrees. Remove from the oven, sprinkle with pepper and lemon juice. Decorate with few parsley leaves. Allow it to cool for about 10 minutes.

Nutritional values per 100g:

Carbohydrates 8.2g

Sugar 4.9g

Protein 22g

Total fat 9.6g

Sodium 97.2 mg

Potassium 381mg

Calcium 4.5mg

Iron 5.3mg

Vitamins (vitamin A; B-6; B-12; C; D; D2; D3; K; Riboflavin; Niacin; Thiamin; K)

Calories 216

32.Tomato soup

Ingredients:

1 cup of tomato sauce

2 egg whites

2 cups of water

2 cloves of garlic

2 tbsp of olive oil

1tsp of dried marjoram

chopped parsley

Preparation:

Fry finely chopped garlic in oil. Stir in tomato sauce mixed with water. Add parsley and let it boil. Serve with marjoram.

Nutritional values per 150ml:

Carbohydrates 6.8g

Sugar 3.9g

Protein 7g

Total fat (good monounsaturated fat) 0.6g

Sodium 190.2 mg

Potassium 112mg

Calcium 0.5mg

Iron 2.3mg

Vitamins (vitamin A; C)

Calories 30

33. Grilled zucchini with chopped basil and mint

Ingredients:

1 large zucchini

¼ cup of chopped basil

¼ cup of chopped mint

1 tbsp of olive oil

¼ glass of water,

pepper to taste

Preparation:

Cook spices in water and add pepper for 2-3 minutes. Peel and cut zucchini into three slices. Grill it in a barbecue pan with olive oil. Add mint and basil. Fry until all the water evaporates. You can add some lemon juice before serving, but this is optional.

Nutritional values for 1 slice:

Carbohydrates 3.8g

Sugar 2g

Protein 2.9 g

Total fat 0.9g

Sodium 2.76 mg

Potassium 343mg

Calcium 0.27mg

Iron 0.3mg

Vitamins (vitamin A; B-6; B-12; C; D:K)

Calories 23

34. Chopped veal soup with vegetables

Ingredients:

1 thick veal steak

2 large carrots

½ cup of chopped parsley

1 large tomato

¼ tsp of pepper

1 small onion

Preparation:

Wash the meat and put it in a pot. Pour water and cook until meat is tender. Meanwhile, clean and cut the vegetables into small cubes. When the meat is cooked, remove it from the pan and cut it into small cubes. Mix with vegetables, return to the water and cook until carrots are tender. Add seasoning and serve.

Nutritional values per 1 cup:

Carbohydrates 3g

Sugar 2.1g

Protein 22 g

Total fat 5.7g

Sodium 71 mg

Potassium 148mg

Calcium 2.2mg

Iron 4.3mg

Vitamins (vitamin A; B-6; B-12; C; D; D2; D3; K; Riboflavin; Niacin; Thiamin; K)

Calories 112

35. Lamb cutlet with hazelnut sauce

Ingredients:

1 medium lamb cutlet

½ cup of hazelnuts

1 tsp of curry

1 tbsp of olive oil

pepper to taste

Preparation:

Wash the cutlet and cook in water 15-20 minutes. Remove from pot and drain, but keep the water. Make a sauce with olive oil, curry, hazelnuts and pepper. Spread the sauce over cutlet, add some meat water and bake at 300 degrees for 15-20 minutes.

Nutritional values per 100g:

Carbohydrates 4.7g

Sugar 4.1g

Protein 29 g

Total fat 11.8g

Sodium 137 mg

Potassium 239mg

Calcium 2.9mg

Iron 2.16mg

Vitamins (vitamin A; B-6; B-12; C; D; D2; D3; K; Riboflavin; Niacin; Thiamin; K)

Calories 213

36.Grilled red pepper

Ingredients:

1 large red pepper

1 tbsp of olive oil

2 cloves of garlic

chopped parsley

Preparation:

Mix olive oil with garlic and parsley. Spread the sauce over paprika and bake in barbecue pan on low temperature for about 10-15 minutes.

Nutritional values per 100g:

Carbohydrates 6.2g

Sugar 4.4g

Protein 2g

Total fat 0.8g

Sodium 7 mg

Potassium 215mg

Calcium 2.8mg

Iron 2. 6mg

Vitamins (vitamin A; B-6; B-12; C; D; Riboflavin; Niacin; Thiamin; K)

Calories 38

37.Eggplant pate

Ingredients:

1 large eggplant

6 egg whites

1 tsp of mustard

1 tsp of non-fat mayonnaise

2 cloves of garlic

1 tsp of parsley

¼ cup of water

1 tsp of olive oil

Preparation:

Note: The amount of eggplant and water can vary greatly depending on the type of eggplant and ways of preparing this pate. Eggplant baked in the oven will be dry, but it will be tastier and less bitter. Eggplant cleaned and "cooked" in a microwave will be lighter, with more fluid and a little more bitter, but ready in no time.

Peel the eggplant, cut into cubes and cook together in a covered, fireproof dish in the microwave for about 5 minutes. Or, bake in a conventional oven, peel the bark, well drain of water. Add water and blend eggplant with stick-blender.

Mix mayonnaise with egg whites and olive oil. Add eggplant and blend it together.

Add finely chopped garlic and mustard. This way you can get approximately one big jar of pate. It is excellent as a spread or as a side dish. Perfect with chicken and turkey.

Nutritional values per 100g:

Carbohydrates 12.9g

Sugar 6g

Protein 17g

Total fat 3.4g

Sodium 154mg

Potassium 132.5mg

Calcium 10.4mg

Iron 3.37mg

Vitamins (vitamin A; B-6; B-12; C; D; D2; D3; K; Riboflavin; Niacin; Thiamin; K)

Calories 71

38. Stewed beef and cabbage

Ingredients:

1 large beefsteak

1 cup of chopped cabbage, cooked

¼ tsp of pepper

2 tbsp of olive oil

½ cup of water

Preparation:

Cut meat into small pieces. Put in a pot and cook on a low temperature, in olive oil until tender. Add some water if necessary. When the meat tender, add cabbage and pepper. Stew on low temperature for at least 40 minutes.

Nutritional values per 100g:

Carbohydrates 8.1g

Sugar 3.2g

Protein 36.1 g

Total fat 6.9g

Sodium 157 mg

Potassium 499mg

Calcium 19.9mg

Iron 5.9mg

Vitamins (vitamin A; B-6; B-12; C; D; D2; D3; K;Thiamin; K)

Calories 234

39. Broccoli soup

Ingredients:

1 cup of broccoli

1 small carrot

1 small onion

little salt

pepper to taste

1 tbsp of coconut oil

Preparation:

Wash the onions and carrots, but do not chop them. Put them together with the broccoli in salted water and cook. When the vegetables are done, put them all together in a blender. Remaining vegetable water heat to boiling point and stir with a little oil. Cook until the mixture thickens, add the vegetables and cook for another 5-7 minutes. Serve warm.

Nutritional values for 1 cup:

Carbohydrates 15g

Sugar 5.2g

Protein 7.2 g

Total fat 4.1g

Sodium 887 mg

Potassium 376mg

Calcium 25.5mg

Iron 1.2mg

Vitamins (vitamin A;C)

Calories 120

40. Lettuce and tuna salad

Ingredients:

1 bunch of lettuce

3 cans of tuna without oil

1 tbsp of lemon juice

2 large onions

2 large tomatoes

5 olives

Preparation:

Wash and cut lettuce. Mix it with tuna. Peel and cut the onion, cut the tomato, mix with tuna and lettuce. Add lemon juice and olives.

Nutritional values for 1 cup:

Carbohydrates 19.4g

Sugar 12g

Protein 31.2g

Total fat (good monounsaturated fat) 11.5g

Sodium 141mg

Potassium 86.1mg

Calcium 43.2mg

Iron 0.31mg

Vitamins (vitamin A; B-6; B-12; C; D; D2; D3; K; Riboflavin; Niacin; Thiamin; K)

Calories 71

41. Grilled trout fillets with parsley

Ingredients:

3 thick trout fillets

1 tbsp of parsley

3 tbsp of olive oil

6 cloves of garlic

Preparation:

Mix chopped garlic with parsley and olive oil. Spread it over fish and fry in a barbecue pan for about 15-20 minutes, on both sides. Remove from the pan and use a kitchen paper to soak the excess oil.

Nutritional values per 100g:

Carbohydrates 0.2g

Sugar 0

Protein 25.2 g

Total fat 6.6g

Sodium 113.8 mg

Potassium 61mg

Calcium 29mg

Iron 0.33mg

Vitamins (vitamin A; B-6; B-12; C; D; D2; D3; K; Riboflavin; Niacin; Thiamin; K)

Calories 170

42. Cauliflower soup

Ingredients:

1 cup of cauliflower

1 small carrot

1 small onion

little pepper

1 tbsp of oil

Preparation:

Wash the onions and carrots, but do not chop them. Put them together with the cauliflower in water and cook. When the vegetables are done, put them all together in a blender. Remaining vegetable water heat to boiling point and stir with a little oil. Cook until the mixture thickens, add the vegetables and cook for another 5-7 minutes. Serve warm.

Nutritional values for 1 cup:

Carbohydrates 13g

Sugar 4.2g

Protein 6.2 g

Total fat 4.4g

Sodium 862 mg

Potassium 366mg

Calcium 24.1mg

Iron 2mg

Vitamins (vitamin A;C)

Calories 118

43.Tomato omelet

Ingredients:

3 eggs

1 large tomato

1 small onion

1 tsp of olive oil

salt to taste

Preparation:

Wash and cut tomato. Peel and cut the onion. Fry tomato and onion in olive oil for about 10-15 minutes, on a low temperature. Remove from the heat when the water evaporates. Add eggs and mix well. Fry for another 2 minutes.

Nutritional values per 100 g:

Carbohydrates 6.1g

Sugar 2g

Protein 20g

Total fat (good monounsaturated fat) 12g

Sodium 176mg

Potassium 173mg

Calcium 15.9mg

Iron 1.9mg

Vitamins (vitamin A; B-6; B-12; C)

Calories 184

44. Grilled salmon fillet

Ingredients:

1 large salmon fillet

1 tbsp of lemon juice

2 tbsp of olive oil

1 tbsp of ground chili pepper

Preparation:

Wash the fillet and pat dry using a kitchen paper. Sprinkle some lemon juice on it and fry in a small barbecue pan for about 15-20 minutes, on a very high temperature. Remove from the pan and soak the excess oil with a kitchen paper. Add ground chili pepper before serving.

Nutritional values per 100 g:

Carbohydrates 2.9

Sugar 0.8g

Protein 24g

Total fat (good monounsaturated fat) 14.6g

Sodium 63mg

Potassium 374mg

Calcium 0.9mg

Iron 1.8mg

Vitamins (vitamin A; B-6; B-12; C)

Calories 220

45.Mixed vegetable salad:

Ingredients:

1 bunch of lettuce

1 small carrot

1 medium tomato

1 medium onion

1 small cucumber

1 medium eggplant

1 medium zucchini

1 tbsp of olive oil

1 tsp of lemon juice

Preparation:

Peel and cut eggplant and zucchini. Fry it in olive oil for 8-10 minutes. Remove from pan and soak excess oil with kitchen paper. Meanwhile, wash and cut vegetables into small pieces. Mix eggplant and zucchini with other vegetables and season with olive oil and lemon juice.

Nutritional values for one cup:

Carbohydrates 12.3g

Sugar 8.9g

Protein 11.2 g

Total fat (good monounsaturated fat) 6.5g

Sodium 176.3 mg

Potassium 95mg

Calcium 63.5mg

Iron 0.74mg

Vitamins (vitamin A; B-6; B-12; C; D; D2; D3; K; Riboflavin; Niacin; Thiamin; K)

Calories 51

POST-COMPETITION SHAKES FOR BODYBUILDING

1. Oat & Almond Shake

Preparing time: 5 minutes
Servings: 3

1. Ingredients:

220ml milk
1 tablespoon almonds (grinded) (15g)
1 tablespoon oats (15g)
1 teaspoon maple syrup (5g)
½ teaspoon vanilla extract (2-3g)
2 tablespoon Greek Yogurt (30g)
30g whey protein

2. Preparation:

All ingredients go in a blender and are blend until the consistence is smooth.

3. Nutritional facts (amount per 100ml/entire composition):

Contains calcium, iron;

Calories: 111	Total Fat: 3.2g
Calories from Fat: 29	Saturated Fat: 0.7g

Cholesterol: 21mg
Sodium: 58mg

Potassium: 182mg

Total Carbohydrates: 9.3g
Dietary Fiber: 0.8g
Sugar: 5.1g
Protein: 11.1g
Calories: 333

Calories from Fat: 86

Total Fat: 9.5g

Saturated Fat: 2.1g

Cholesterol: 64mg

Sodium: 175mg

Potassium: 547mg

Total Carbohydrates: 27.9g
Dietary Fiber: 2.6g
Sugar: 15.3g
Protein: 33.5g

2. Peppermint Oatmeal Shake

Preparing time: 5 minutes
Servings: 5

1. Ingredients:

70g oatmeal
30g bran flakes
300ml milk
50g quark
½ teaspoon peppermint extract (3g)
30g ice-cream (vanilla/chocolate)
50g whey protein (chocolate)

2. Preparation:

Mix all ingredients in a blender until the composition is smooth.

3. Nutritional facts (amount per 100ml/entire composition):

Contains Vitamin A, calcium, iron.

Calories: 180
Calories from Fat: 51

Total Fat: 5.6g
Saturated Fat: 2.9g

Cholesterol: 30mg
Sodium: 111mg

Potassium: 179mg

Total Carbohydrates: 20.7g
Dietary Fiber: 2.5g

Sugar: 6.2g
Protein: 12.6g
Calories: 900

Calories from Fat: 253

Total Fat: 28.1g

Saturated Fat: 14.4g

Cholesterol: 151mg

Sodium: 555mg

Potassium: 869mg

Total Carbohydrates: 104g

Dietary Fiber: 12.4g

Sugar: 31.2g

Protein: 63.2g

3. Cinnamon Shake

Preparing time: 5 minutes
Servings: 3

1. Ingredients:

240ml milk
¼ tablespoon cinnamon (4g)
½ teaspoon vanilla extracts (3g)
2 tablespoon vanilla ice-cream (30g)
2 tablespoon oats (30g)
50g whey protein

2. Preparation:

Mix all ingredients in a blender until the composition is smooth.

3. Nutritional facts (amount per 100g/entire composition):

Contains Vitamin A, calcium, iron.

Calories: 131
- Calories from Fat: 30

Total Fat: 3.3g
- Saturated Fat: 1.8g

Cholesterol: 42mg
Sodium: 73mg

Potassium: 158mg

Total Carbohydrates: 10.3g
- Dietary Fiber: 1g

Sugar: 4.8g
Protein: 15.3g
Calories: 342

Calories from Fat: 89

Total Fat: 9.9g

Saturated Fat: 5.4g

Cholesterol: 127mg

Sodium: 219mg

Potassium: 474mg

Total Carbohydrates: 31g
Dietary Fiber: 3.1g
Sugar: 14.4g
Protein: 45.9g

4. Almonds Shake

Preparing time: 5 minutes
Servings: 5

1. Ingredients:

220ml almond milk
120g oatmeal
50g whey protein
80g raisins
20g almonds (grinded)
1 tablespoon peanut butter (15g)

2. Preparation:

Mix all ingredients in a blender until the composition is smooth.

3. Nutritional facts (amount per 100g/entire composition):

Contains : Vitamin C, iron, calcium.

Calories: 241
- Calories from Fat: 61

Total Fat: 6.7g
- Saturated Fat: 1.6g

Cholesterol: 24mg
Sodium: 57mg

Potassium: 339mg

Total Carbohydrates: 33.8g
- Dietary Fiber: 3.7g

Sugar: 12.5g
Protein: 13.9g
Calories: 1207

Calories from Fat: 304

Total Fat: 33.7g

Saturated Fat: 8g

Cholesterol: 122mg

Sodium: 283mg

Potassium: 1693mg

Total Carbohydrates: 169g

Dietary Fiber: 18.5g

Sugar: 62.3g

Protein: 69.4g

5. Banana & Almonds Shake

Preparing time: 5 minutes
Servings: 5

1. Ingredients:

2 bananas
230ml almond milk
20g almonds (grinded)
10g pistachios (grinded)
40g whey protein

2. Preparation:

Mix all ingredients in a blender until the composition is smooth.

3. Nutritional facts (amount per 100g/entire composition):

Contains Vitamin A, C, iron, calcium.

Calories: 241
Calories from Fat: 61

Total Fat: 6.7g
Saturated Fat: 1.6g

Cholesterol: 24mg
Sodium: 57mg

Potassium: 339mg

Total Carbohydrates: 33.8g
Dietary Fiber: 3.7g

Sugar: 12.5g
Protein: 13.9g
Calories: 1073

Calories from Fat: 659

Total Fat: 73.2g

Saturated Fat: 52.1g

Cholesterol: 83mg

Sodium: 109mg

Potassium: 1934mg

Total Carbohydrates: 78.7g

Dietary Fiber: 14.8g

Sugar: 39.4g

Protein: 42.8g

6. Wild Berry Shake

Preparing time: 5 minutes
Servings: 7

1. Ingredients:

30g strawberries
30g blueberries
30g raspberries
30g currants
500ml milk
60g whey protein
1 teaspoon vanilla extract (5g)
1 teaspoon lemon extract (5g)

2. Preparation:

Mix all ingredients in a blender until the composition is smooth. You can also add some ice cubes to the mix.

3. Nutritional facts (amount per 100g/entire composition):

Contains Vitamin A, C, iron, calcium.

Calories: 78
Calories from Fat: 19

Total Fat: 2.1g
Saturated Fat: 1.2g

Cholesterol: 24mg
Sodium: 50mg

Potassium: 119mg

Total Carbohydrates:
6.7g
Dietary Fiber: 0.7g
Sugar: 4.7g
Protein: 8.7g
Calories: 549

Calories from Fat:
131

Total Fat: 14.6g

Saturated Fat:
8.1g

Cholesterol: 167mg

Sodium: 351mg

Potassium: 832mg

Total Carbohydrates:
46.9g
Dietary Fiber: 4.6g
Sugar: 33g
Protein: 61g

7. Strawberry Shake

Preparing time: 5 minutes
Servings: 5

1. Ingredients:

30g strawberries
100g Greek Yogurt
200ml milk
40g whey protein
2 eggs
20g sweetener (honey/ brown sugar)
ice cubes
1 teaspoon vanilla extract (5g)

2. Preparation:

Mix all ingredients in a blender until the composition is smooth.

The Greek Yogurt can have different aromas like vanilla or strawberry, or just be plain yogurt. It works will all flavors.

3. Nutritional facts (amount per 100g/entire composition):

Contains Vitamin A, C, iron, calcium.
Calories: 96 Calories from Fat: 32

Total Fat: 3.5g
Saturated Fat: 1.6g

Cholesterol: 87mg
Sodium: 65mg

Potassium: 131mg

Total Carbohydrates: 9.2g
Dietary Fiber: 2.5g
Sugar: 3.4g
Protein: 11.3g

Calories: 508

Calories from Fat: 157

Total Fat: 17.4g

Saturated Fat: 8g

Cholesterol: 433mg

Sodium: 326mg

Potassium: 656mg

Total Carbohydrates: 45.9g
Dietary Fiber: 12.4g
Sugar: 17.2g
Protein: 56.6g

8. Strawberry Vanilla Shake

Preparing time: 5 minutes
Servings: 7

1. Ingredients:

100g strawberries
1 banana
1 teaspoon vanilla extract (5g)
1 tablespoon strawberries extract (15g)
50g oats
200ml milk
5 eggs
Ice cubes

2. Preparation:

Mix all ingredients in a blender until the composition is smooth.

3. Nutritional facts (amount per 100g/entire composition):

Contains Vitamin A, C, iron, calcium.

Calories: 112

Calories from Fat: 39

Total Fat: 4.3g

Saturated Fat: 1.4g

Cholesterol: 119mg

Sodium: 59mg

Potassium: 170mg

Total Carbohydrates: 11.7g

Dietary Fiber: 1.4g

Sugar: 4.6g

Protein: 6.1g

Calories: 782

Calories from Fat: 271

Total Fat: 30.1g

Saturated Fat: 10.1g

Cholesterol: 835mg

Sodium: 421mg

Potassium: 1189mg

Total Carbohydrates: 82g

Dietary Fiber: 10.1g

Sugar: 32.5g

Protein: 43g

9. Strawberry & Nuts Shake

Preparing time: 5 minutes
Servings: 4

1. Ingredients:

50g strawberries
50g mix nuts (chopped)
200ml milk
100g Greek yogurt
2 tablespoon oats (30g)

2. Preparation:

Mix all ingredients in a blender until the composition is smooth.

3. Nutritional facts (amount per 100g/entire composition):

Contains Vitamin A, C, iron, calcium.

Calories: 140
Calories from Fat: 81

Total Fat: 9g
Saturated Fat: 1.4g

Cholesterol: 1mg

Sodium: 80mg

Potassium: 125mg

Total Carbohydrates: 9.2g
Dietary Fiber: 1.4g
Sugar: 4.3g

Protein: 6.9g

Calories: 417

Calories from Fat: 324

Total Fat: 36g

Saturated Fat: 5.4g

Cholesterol: 5mg

Sodium: 321mg

Potassium: 499mg

Total Carbohydrates: 36.9g

Dietary Fiber: 5.5g

Sugar: 17.1g

Protein: 27.6g

10. Raspberry Shake

Preparing time: 5 minutes
Servings: 4

1. Ingredients:

50g whey protein
100g raspberries
30g strawberries
50g sour cream
200ml milk
1 teaspoon lime extract (5g)

2. Preparation:

Mix all ingredients in a blender until the composition is smooth.

3. Nutritional facts (amount per 100g/entire composition):

Contains Vitamin A, C, B-12, iron, calcium.

Calories: 116
- Calories from Fat: 41

Total Fat: 4.6g
- Saturated Fat: 2.6g

Cholesterol: 36mg
Sodium: 54mg

Potassium: 168mg

Total Carbohydrates: 8.1g
- Dietary Fiber: 1.8g

Sugar: 4.2g
Protein: 11.4g
Calories: 465

Calories from Fat: 166

Total Fat: 18.4g

Saturated Fat: 10.6g

Cholesterol: 143mg

Sodium: 214mg

Potassium: 670mg

Total Carbohydrates: 32.5g
Dietary Fiber: 7.1g
Sugar: 16.8g
Protein: 45.5g

11. Blueberry Shake

Preparing time: 5 minutes
Servings: 6

1. ***Ingredients:***

250g blueberries
50g sour cream
80g oats
100ml coconut milk
160g pumpkin puree
Cinnamon, nutmeg for sprinkle on top

2. ***Preparation:***

Mix all ingredients in a blender until the composition is smooth.

3. ***Nutritional facts (amount per 100g/entire composition):***

Contains Vitamin A, C, iron, calcium.

Calories: 140
- Calories from Fat: 62

Total Fat: 6.9g
- Saturated Fat: 4.8g

Cholesterol: 4mg
Sodium: 9mg

Potassium: 192mg

Total Carbohydrates: 18.5g
- Dietary Fiber: 3.5g

Sugar: 5.7g
Protein: 3g
Calories: 641

Calories from Fat: 371

Total Fat: 41.2g

Saturated Fat: 29.1g

Cholesterol: 22mg

Sodium: 56mg

Potassium: 1150mg

Total Carbohydrates: 112g
Dietary Fiber: 21g
Sugar: 34.4g
Protein: 18.1g

12. Peanut Butter Shake

Preparing time: 5 minutes
Servings: 6

1. Ingredients:

300ml almond milk
50g peanut butter
50g mix nuts
6 egg whites
1 teaspoon butter extract (5g)

2. Preparation:

Mix all ingredients in a blender until the composition is smooth.

3. Nutritional facts (amount per 100g/entire composition):

Contains Vitamin C, iron, calcium.

Calories: 236
Calories from Fat: 191

Total Fat: 21.3g
Saturated Fat: 12.2g

Cholesterol: 0mg

Sodium: 109mg

Potassium: 241mg

Total Carbohydrates: 6.2g
Dietary Fiber: 2g
Sugar: 3.1g

Protein: 8.3g

Calories: 1415

Calories from Fat: 1148

Total Fat: 127.6g

Saturated Fat: 73.1g

Cholesterol: 0mg

Sodium: 656mg

Potassium: 1448mg

Total Carbohydrates: 37.2g

Dietary Fiber: 11.9g

Sugar: 18.5g

Protein: 50.2g

13. Peanut Butter & Banana Shake

Preparing time: 5 minutes
Servings: 7

1. Ingredients:

250ml almond milk
2 bananas
30g peanut butter
5 eggs
2 teaspoons honey (10g)
1 teaspoon vanilla extract (5g)

2. Preparation:

Mix all ingredients in a blender until the composition is smooth.

3. Nutritional facts (amount per 100g/entire composition):

Contains Vitamin A, C, iron, calcium.

Calories: 191
  Calories from Fat: 126

Total Fat: 14g
  Saturated Fat: 9.1g

Cholesterol: 117mg
Sodium: 70mg

Potassium: 288mg

Total Carbohydrates: 12.5g
  Dietary Fiber: 1.9g

Sugar: 7.7g
Protein: 6.2g
Calories: 1339

Calories from Fat: 884

Total Fat: 98.2g

Saturated Fat: 63.9g

Cholesterol: 818mg

Sodium: 487mg

Potassium: 2015mg

Total Carbohydrates: 87.6g
Dietary Fiber: 13.5g
Sugar: 53.9g
Protein: 43.6g

14. Peanut Butter & Chocolate Shake

Preparing time: 5 minutes
Servings: 3

1. Ingredients:

2 tablespoon cocoa powder (30g)
30g peanut butter
250ml almond milk
50g whey protein

2. Preparation:

Mix all ingredients in a blender until the composition is smooth.

3. Nutritional facts (amount per 100g/entire composition):

Contains Vitamin C, iron, calcium.

Calories: 326
- Calories from Fat: 240

Total Fat: 26.6g
- Saturated Fat: 19.7g

Cholesterol: 35mg
Sodium: 89mg
Potassium: 472mg

Total Carbohydrates: 10.6g
- Dietary Fiber: 3.5g
- Sugar: 4.3g

Protein: 17g
Calories: 977

Calories from Fat: 719

Total Fat: 79.9g

Saturated Fat: 59.1g

Cholesterol: 104mg

Sodium: 267mg

Potassium: 1415mg

Total Carbohydrates: 31.8g

Dietary Fiber: 10.6g

Sugar: 13g

Protein: 51g

15. Chocolate Shake

Preparing time: 5 minutes
Servings: 6

1. Ingredients:

3 tablespoon cocoa powder (45g)
250ml milk
120ml pumpkin puree
1 teaspoon vanilla extract (5g)
5 eggs

2. Preparation:

Mix all ingredients in a blender until the composition is smooth.

3. Nutritional facts (amount per 100g/entire composition):

Contains Vitamin A, C, iron, calcium

Calories: 89

Calories from Fat: 44

Total Fat: 4.9g

Saturated Fat: 1.9g

Cholesterol: 140mg

Sodium: 73mg

Potassium: 185mg

Total Carbohydrates: 5.6g

Dietary Fiber: 1.4g

Sugar: 3g

Protein: 6.7g
Calories: 534

Calories from Fat: 267

Total Fat: 29.6g

Saturated Fat: 11.4g

Cholesterol: 840mg

Sodium: 439mg

Potassium: 1112mg

Total Carbohydrates: 33.8g

Dietary Fiber: 8.4g

Sugar: 18.2g

Protein: 40.4g

16. Chocolate & Almond

Preparing time: 5 minutes
Servings: 5

1. Ingredients:

2 tablespoon chocolate pudding (30g)
50g almond (chopped)
300ml milk
40g whey protein
1 teaspoon amaretto syrup (5g)

2. Preparation:

Mix all ingredients in a blender until the composition is smooth.

3. Nutritional facts (amount per 100g/entire composition):

Contains Vitamin A, iron, calcium.

Calories: 131

Calories from Fat: 61

Total Fat: 6.8g

Saturated Fat: 1.4g

Cholesterol: 22mg

Sodium: 70mg

Potassium: 154mg

Total Carbohydrates: 9g

Dietary Fiber: 1.3g

Sugar: 3.5g

Protein: 9.9g
Calories: 656

Calories from Fat: 303

Total Fat: 33.7g

Saturated Fat: 6.9g

Cholesterol: 109mg

Sodium: 351mg

Potassium: 770mg

Total Carbohydrates: 45.2g

Dietary Fiber: 6.5g

Sugar: 17.2g

Protein: 49.3g

17. Caramel and Hazelnuts Shake

Preparing time: 5 minutes
Servings: 4

1. Ingredients:

50g hazelnuts (chopped)
1 teaspoon caramel syrup (5g)
1 teaspoon maple syrup (5g)
250ml almond milk
50g whey protein

2. Preparation:

Mix all ingredients in a blender until the composition is smooth.

3. Nutritional facts (amount per 100g/entire composition):

Contains Vitamin C, iron, calcium.

Calories: 307

- Calories from Fat: 211

Total Fat: 23.4g

- Saturated Fat: 14.3g

Cholesterol: 26mg

Sodium: 37mg

Potassium: 326mg

Total Carbohydrates: 15.5g

- Dietary Fiber: 2.6g
- Sugar: 11g

Protein: 12.2g
Calories: 1228

Calories from Fat: 844

Total Fat: 93.8g

Saturated Fat: 57.3g

Cholesterol: 104mg

Sodium: 148mg

Potassium: 1303mg

Total Carbohydrates: 61.8g

Dietary Fiber: 10.4g

Sugar: 44.1g

Protein: 49g

18. Plum Shake

Preparing time: 5 minutes
Servings: 8

1. Ingredients:

200g plum
50g raisin
200ml milk
4 eggs
100g quark
70g oats

2. Preparation:

Mix all ingredients in a blender until the composition is smooth.

3. Nutritional facts (amount per 100g/entire composition):

Contains Vitamin A, C, iron, calcium.

Calories: 122

Calories from Fat: 43

Total Fat: 4.7g

Saturated Fat: 1.8g

Cholesterol: 87mg

Sodium: 62mg

Potassium: 149mg

Total Carbohydrates: 14.7g
Dietary Fiber: 1.3g
Sugar: 7.2g
Protein: 6.2g
Calories: 975

Calories from Fat: 340

Total Fat: 37.8g

Saturated Fat: 14.3g

Cholesterol: 699mg

Sodium: 499mg

Potassium: 1190mg

Total Carbohydrates: 117g
Dietary Fiber: 10.7g
Sugar: 57.7g
Protein: 49.7g

19. Tropical Shake

Preparing time: 5 minutes
Servings: 5

1. Ingredients:

1 banana
150g pineapple
40g mango
200ml coconut milk
1 teaspoon honey (5g)
50g whey protein

2. Preparation:

Mix all ingredients in a blender until the composition is smooth.

3. Nutritional facts (amount per 100g/entire composition):

Contains Vitamin A, C, iron, calcium.

Calories: 178

Calories from Fat: 94

Total Fat: 10.4g

Saturated Fat: 8.9g

Cholesterol: 21mg

Sodium: 25mg

Potassium: 294mg

Total Carbohydrates: 15.3g
- Dietary Fiber: 2.1g
- Sugar: 9.9g

Protein: 8.5g

Calories: 889

- Calories from Fat: 468

Total Fat: 52g

- Saturated Fat: 44.6g

Cholesterol: 104mg

Sodium: 124mg

Potassium: 1468mg

Total Carbohydrates: 76.4g
- Dietary Fiber: 10.3g
- Sugar: 49.2g

Protein: 42.7g

20. Peach Shake
Preparing time: 5 minutes
Servings: 8

1. ***Ingredients:***

6 peaches
300ml milk
140g mandarins
30g oats
4 eggs

2. ***Preparation:***

Mix all ingredients in a blender until the composition is smooth.

3. ***Nutritional facts (amount per 100g/entire composition):***

Contains Vitamin A, C, iron, calcium.

Calories: 70
- Calories from Fat: 20

Total Fat: 2.3g
- Saturated Fat: 0.3g

Cholesterol: 57mg

Sodium: 34mg

Potassium: 137mg

Total Carbohydrates: 9.5g
- Dietary Fiber: 1g
- Sugar: 7.2g

Protein: 3.5g
Calories: 839

Calories from Fat: 245

Total Fat: 27.3g

Saturated Fat: 9.7g

Cholesterol: 680mg

Sodium: 405mg

Potassium: 1639mg

Total Carbohydrates: 115g

Dietary Fiber: 12.4g

Sugar: 86.2g

Protein: 41.6g

21.Plum & Lemon Shake
Preparing time: 5 minutes
Servings: 6

1. Ingredients:

150g plums
2 lemons (juice)
2 teaspoons honey (10g)
200ml milk
Ice cubes
150g Greek Yogurt
4 eggs

2. Preparation:

Mix all ingredients in a blender until the composition is smooth.

3. Nutritional facts (amount per 100g/entire composition):

Contains Vitamin A, C, iron, calcium.
Calories: 74

Calories from Fat: 29

Total Fat: 3.2g

Saturated Fat: 1.3g

Cholesterol: 85mg

Sodium: 50mg

Potassium: 111mg

Total Carbohydrates: 6.4g
- Dietary Fiber: 0.6g
- Sugar: 5.1g

Protein: 5.8g

Calories: 589

Calories from Fat: 228

Total Fat: 25.3g

Saturated Fat: 10.3g

Cholesterol: 679mg

Sodium: 397mg

Potassium: 890mg

Total Carbohydrates: 51.2g
- Dietary Fiber: 4.6g
- Sugar: 40.9g

Protein: 45.9g

22. Pineapple Shake

Preparing time: 5 minutes
Servings: 6

1. Ingredients:

300g pineapple
200ml almond milk
30g raspberries
30g oats
1 lime (juice)
40g whey protein

2. Preparation:

Mix all ingredients in a blender until the composition is smooth.

3. Nutritional facts (amount per 100g/entire composition):

Contains Vitamin A, C, iron, calcium.

Calories: 153

Calories from Fat: 80

Total Fat: 8.9g

Saturated Fat: 7.4g

Cholesterol: 14mg

Sodium: 18mg

Potassium: 218mg

Total Carbohydrates: 14.4g

Dietary Fiber: 2.6g

Sugar: 6.7g

Protein: 6.6g

Calories: 920

Calories from Fat: 481

Total Fat: 53.4g

Saturated Fat: 44.5g

Cholesterol: 83mg

Sodium: 109mg

Potassium: 1309mg

Total Carbohydrates: 86.3g

Dietary Fiber: 15.5g

Sugar: 40.3g

Protein: 39.6g

23. Orange Shake
Preparing time: 5 minutes
Servings: 8

1. ***Ingredients:***

5 oranges
10 eggs
2 tablespoon honey

2. ***Preparation:***

Mix all ingredients in a blender until the composition is smooth.

3. ***Nutritional facts (amount per 100g/entire composition):***

Contains Vitamin A, C, iron, calcium.
Calories: 85

Calories from Fat: 29

Total Fat: 3.2g

Saturated Fat: 1g

Cholesterol: 117mg

Sodium: 44mg

Potassium: 163mg

Total Carbohydrates: 10.4g
Dietary Fiber: 1.6g
Sugar: 8.8g
Protein: 4.6g
Calories: 1189

Calories from Fat: 404

Total Fat: 44.8g

Saturated Fat: 13.8g

Cholesterol: 1637mg

Sodium: 618mg

Potassium: 2277mg

Total Carbohydrates: 146g

Dietary Fiber: 22.2g

Sugar: 123.9g

Protein: 64.1g

24. Pinna Colada Shake

Preparing time: 5 minutes
Servings: 8

1. Ingredients:

200g pineapple
200g coconut milk
50g oats
300ml milk
4 eggs

2. Preparation:

Mix all ingredients in a blender until the composition is smooth.

3. Nutritional facts (amount per 100g/entire composition):

Contains Vitamin A, C, iron, calcium.

Calories: 128

Calories from Fat: 75

Total Fat: 8.3g

Saturated Fat: 5.8g

Cholesterol: 76mg

Sodium: 48mg

Potassium: 149mg

Total Carbohydrates: 9.8g

Dietary Fiber: 1.1g

Sugar: 4.7g

Protein: 4.9g
Calories: 1155

Calories from Fat: 675

Total Fat: 75g

Saturated Fat: 52.1g

Cholesterol: 680mg

Sodium: 428mg

Potassium: 1339mg

Total Carbohydrates: 87.8g

Dietary Fiber: 12.2g

Sugar: 42.2g

Protein: 44.5g

25. Apple Shake
Preparing time: 5 minutes
Servings: 3

1. ***Ingredients:***

350g apple
1 teaspoon cinnamon
200ml almond milk
2 teaspoon vanilla extract
40g whey protein

2. ***Preparation:***

Mix all ingredients in a blender until the composition is smooth.

3. ***Nutritional facts (amount per 100g/entire composition):***

Contains Vitamin C, iron, calcium.
Calories: 139

Calories from Fat: 77

Total Fat: 8.6g

Saturated Fat: 7.4g

Cholesterol: 14mg

Sodium: 18mg

Potassium: 193mg

Total Carbohydrates: 11.2g
Dietary Fiber: 2.3g
Sugar: 7.6g

Protein: 5.7g
Calories: 833

Calories from Fat: 463

Total Fat: 51.4g

Saturated Fat: 44.1g

Cholesterol: 83mg

Sodium: 106mg

Potassium: 1157mg

Total Carbohydrates: 67.3g

Dietary Fiber: 14.2g

Sugar: 45.5g

Protein: 34.3g

26. Egg Shake

Preparing time: 5 minutes
Servings: 8

1. Ingredients:

10 eggs
300ml milk
100g Greek Yogurt
2 tablespoon honey (30g)
50g oats

2. Preparation:

Mix all ingredients in a blender until the composition is smooth.

3. Nutritional facts (amount per 100g/entire composition):

Contains Vitamin A, iron, calcium.

Calories: 131

Calories from Fat: 55

Total Fat: 6.1g

Saturated Fat: 2.2g

Cholesterol: 185mg

Sodium: 89mg

Potassium: 123mg

Total Carbohydrates: 10.1g

Dietary Fiber: 0.6g

Sugar: 6.3g

Protein: 9.1g
Calories: 1176

Calories from Fat: 498

Total Fat: 55.3g

Saturated Fat: 19.5g

Cholesterol: 1667mg

Sodium: 799mg

Potassium: 1111mg

Total Carbohydrates: 91.1g
Dietary Fiber: 5.1g
Sugar: 56.3g
Protein: 82.2g

27. Pumpkin Shake

Preparing time: 5 minutes
Servings: 6

1. ***Ingredients:***

300g pumpkin
300g raspberries
50g sour cream
200ml almond milk
40g whey protein

2. ***Preparation:***

Mix all ingredients in a blender until the composition is smooth.

3. ***Nutritional facts (amount per 100g/entire composition):***

Contains Vitamin A, C, iron, calcium.

Calories: 123

Calories from Fat: 72

Total Fat: 8g

Saturated Fat: 6.4g

Cholesterol: 13mg

Sodium: 18mg

Potassium: 238mg

Total Carbohydrates: 9.8g

Dietary Fiber: 4.1g

Sugar: 3.9g

Protein: 5.2g
Calories: 986

Calories from Fat: 576

Total Fat: 64g

Saturated Fat: 51.1g

Cholesterol: 105mg

Sodium: 146mg

Potassium: 1903mg

Total Carbohydrates: 78.2g

Dietary Fiber: 32.7g

Sugar: 31.2g

Protein: 41.7g

28. Beets Shake

Preparing time: 5 minutes
Servings: 6

1. Ingredients:

300g beets
50g parsley
80g blueberries
200ml milk
60g whey protein

2. Preparation:

Mix all ingredients in a blender until the composition is smooth.

3. Nutritional facts (amount per 100g/entire composition):

Contains Vitamin A, C, iron, calcium.

Calories: 89

Calories from Fat: 14

Total Fat: 1.5g

Saturated Fat: 0.7g

Cholesterol: 24mg

Sodium: 77mg

Potassium: 285mg

Total Carbohydrates: 10.3g
Dietary Fiber: 1.6g
Sugar: 7.2g

Protein: 9.5g
Calories: 531

Calories from Fat: 81

Total Fat: 9g

Saturated Fat: 4.5g

Cholesterol: 142mg

Sodium: 464mg

Potassium: 1711mg

Total Carbohydrates: 61.9g
Dietary Fiber: 9.6g
Sugar: 43.3g
Protein: 56.8g

29. Coconut Shake

Preparing time: 5 minutes
Servings: 5

1. Ingredients:

100ml coconut milk
200ml milk
100g Greek Yogurt
50g whey protein
1 teaspoon coconut extract
30g coconut flakes

2. Preparation:

Mix all ingredients in a blender until the composition is smooth.

3. Nutritional facts (amount per 100g/entire composition):

Contains Vitamin A, C, iron, calcium.

Calories: 145

Calories from Fat: 78

Total Fat: 8.7g

Saturated Fat: 7.2g

Cholesterol: 25mg

Sodium: 48mg

Potassium: 184mg

Total Carbohydrates: 6.2g
Dietary Fiber: 1g
Sugar: 4.1g
Protein: 11.1g
Calories: 723

Calories from Fat: 391

Total Fat: 43.4g

Saturated Fat: 35.9g

Cholesterol: 126mg

Sodium: 241mg

Potassium: 922mg

Total Carbohydrates: 30.8g
Dietary Fiber: 4.9g
Sugar: 20.6g
Protein: 55.8g

30. Mango Shake

Preparing time: 5 minutes
Servings: 8

1. Ingredients:

3 mango fruits
1 banana
50g strawberries
300ml milk
1 lime juice
6 eggs

2. Preparation:

Mix all ingredients in a blender until the composition is smooth.

3. Nutritional facts (amount per 100g/entire composition):

Contains Vitamin A, C, iron, calcium.

Calories: 87

Calories from Fat: 31

Total Fat: 3.4g

Saturated Fat: 1.2g

Cholesterol: 101mg

Sodium: 52mg

Potassium: 155mg

Total Carbohydrates:
10.3g
Dietary Fiber: 1g
Sugar: 7.8g
Protein: 4.7g
Calories: 874

Calories from Fat:
306

Total Fat: 34g

Saturated Fat:
12.3g

Cholesterol: 1007mg

Sodium: 524mg

Potassium: 1549mg

Total Carbohydrates:
103g
Dietary Fiber: 9.7g
Sugar: 78.5g
Protein: 46.7g

31. Watermelon Shake
Preparing time: 5 minutes
Servings: 6

1. ***Ingredients:***

300g watermelon
200g cantaloupe
200ml water
1 teaspoon vanillas extract
50g sour cream
50g whey protein

2. ***Preparation:***

Mix all ingredients in a blender until the composition is smooth.

3. ***Nutritional facts (amount per 100g/entire composition):***

Contains Vitamin A, C, iron, calcium.

Calories: 59

Calories from Fat: 16

Total Fat: 1.8g

Saturated Fat: 1g

Cholesterol: 16mg

Sodium: 20mg

Potassium: 154mg

Total Carbohydrates: 5.9g

Dietary Fiber: 0g

Sugar: 4.5g
Protein: 5.1g

Calories: 471

Calories from Fat: 128

Total Fat: 14.2g

Saturated Fat: 8.3g

Cholesterol: 126mg

Sodium: 158mg

Potassium: 1230mg

Total Carbohydrates: 47.5g
Dietary Fiber: 3g
Sugar: 36.2g
Protein: 40.7g

32. Greek Yogurt Shake

Preparing time: 5 minutes
Servings: 6

1. Ingredients:

300g Greek Yogurt
100g coconut milk
2 tablespoon honey (30g)
40g raisin
200ml almond milk

2. Preparation:

Mix all ingredients in a blender until the composition is smooth.

3. Nutritional facts (amount per 100g/entire composition):

Contains Vitamin A, C, iron, calcium.

Calories: 167

Calories from Fat: 101

Total Fat: 11.2g

Saturated Fat: 9.8g

Cholesterol: 2mg

Sodium: 21mg

Potassium: 220mg

Total Carbohydrates: 13.6g

Dietary Fiber: 1.2g

Sugar: 11.5g

Protein: 5.5g
Calories: 1169

Calories from Fat: 706

Total Fat: 78.4g

Saturated Fat: 68.5g

Cholesterol: 15mg

Sodium: 149mg

Potassium: 1541mg

Total Carbohydrates: 95.1g
Dietary Fiber: 8.2g
Sugar: 80.3g
Protein: 38.3g

33. Coffee & Banana Shake
Preparing time: 5 minutes
Servings: 6

1. ***Ingredients:***

25g coffee (grinder)
2 bananas
150ml almond milk
20g peanut butter
100ml water
5 eggs

2. ***Preparation:***

Mix all ingredients in a blender until the composition is smooth.

3. ***Nutritional facts (amount per 100g/entire composition):***

Contains Vitamin A, C, iron, calcium.
Calories: 142

Calories from Fat: 89

Total Fat: 9.9g

Saturated Fat: 5.9g

Cholesterol: 117mg

Sodium: 61mg

Potassium: 240mg

Total Carbohydrates: 9.7g
- Dietary Fiber: 1.5g
- Sugar: 5.4g

Protein: 5.5g

Calories: 992

- Calories from Fat: 621

Total Fat: 69g

- Saturated Fat: 41.4g

Cholesterol: 818mg

Sodium: 429mg

Potassium: 1683mg

Total Carbohydrates: 68g
- Dietary Fiber: 10.7g
- Sugar: 37.5g

Protein: 38.8g

34. Spinach Shake

Preparing time: 5 minutes

Servings: 7

1. ***Ingredients:***

200g spinach
50g parsley
70g raspberries
200ml milk
100ml water
50g sour cream
50g whey protein

2. ***Preparation:***

Mix all ingredients in a blender until the composition is smooth.

3. ***Nutritional facts (amount per 100g/entire composition):***

Contains Vitamin A, C, iron, calcium.

Calories: 72

Calories from Fat: 25

Total Fat: 2.8g

Saturated Fat: 1.5g

Cholesterol: 20mg

Sodium: 58mg

Potassium: 282mg

Total Carbohydrates: 5.3g

Dietary Fiber: 1.5g

Sugar: 2.2g

Protein: 7.4g

Calories: 504

Calories from Fat: 174

Total Fat: 19.3g

Saturated Fat: 10.8g

Cholesterol: 143mg

Sodium: 403mg

Potassium: 1973mg

Total Carbohydrates: 37g

Dietary Fiber: 10.6g

Sugar: 15.2g

Protein: 52.1g

35. Chia Shake
Preparing time: 5 minutes
Servings: 5

1. Ingredients:

100g chia seeds
200ml almond milk
50 sour cream
50g parsley
100ml water
40g whey protein

2. Preparation:

Mix all ingredients in a blender until the composition is smooth.

3. Nutritional facts (amount per 100g/entire composition):

Contains Vitamin A, C, iron, calcium.

Calories: 174

Calories from Fat: 123

Total Fat: 13.7g

Saturated Fat: 10g

Cholesterol: 20mg

Sodium: 30mg

Potassium: 260mg

Total Carbohydrates: 6.2g

Dietary Fiber: 3.3g

Sugar: 1.7g
Protein: 8.4g
Calories: 872

Calories from Fat: 615

Total Fat: 68.3g

Saturated Fat: 50.1g

Cholesterol: 99mg

Sodium: 152mg

Potassium: 1300mg

Total Carbohydrates: 31.2g
Dietary Fiber: 16.5g
Sugar: 8.5g
Protein: 42.1g

36. Papaya Shake

Preparing time: 5 minutes
Servings: 6

1. Ingredients:

3 papaya fruits
50g oats
300ml milk
1 teaspoon vanillas extract
50g whey protein

2. Preparation:

Mix all ingredients in a blender until the composition is smooth.

3. Nutritional facts (amount per 100g/entire composition):

Contains Vitamin A, C, iron, calcium.

Calories: 95

Calories from Fat: 14

Total Fat: 1.6g

Saturated Fat: 0.7g

Cholesterol: 16mg

Sodium: 34mg

Potassium: 81mg

Total Carbohydrates: 14.1g

Dietary Fiber: 1.4g

Sugar: 5.4g

Protein: 6.5g
Calories: 760

Calories from Fat: 113

Total Fat: 12.6g

Saturated Fat: 5.9g

Cholesterol: 130mg

Sodium: 268mg

Potassium: 648mg

Total Carbohydrates: 113g

Dietary Fiber: 11.1g

Sugar: 43.5g

Protein: 52.4g

37. Vanilla & Avocado Shake
Preparing time: 5 minutes
Servings: 8

1. ***Ingredients:***

3 avocados
20g vanilla sugar
150ml milk
200ml water
1 teaspoon vanilla extract
40g whey protein (vanilla)

2. ***Preparation:***

Mix all ingredients in a blender until the composition is smooth.

3. ***Nutritional facts (amount per 100g/entire composition):***

Contains Vitamin A, C, iron, calcium.
Calories: 155

Calories from Fat: 111

Total Fat: 12.3g

Saturated Fat: 2.8g

Cholesterol: 10mg

Sodium: 19mg

Potassium: 325mg

Total Carbohydrates:
8.5g
Dietary Fiber: 4g
Sugar: 3.2g
Protein: 4.5g
Calories: 1549

Calories from Fat: 1108

Total Fat: 123.1g

Saturated Fat: 27.8g

Cholesterol: 96mg

Sodium: 187mg

Potassium: 3248mg

Total Carbohydrates:
84.8g
Dietary Fiber: 40.4g
Sugar: 31.7g
Protein: 45.1g

38. Cherry & Almonds Shake

Preparing time: 5 minutes
Servings: 8

1. Ingredients:

300g cherries
100g almond milk
6 eggs
30g almonds (chopped)
75g sour cream
200g milk
1 tablespoon vanillas extract

2. Preparation:

Mix all ingredients in a blender until the composition is smooth.

3. Nutritional facts (amount per 100g/entire composition):

Contains Vitamin A, C, iron, calcium.

Calories: 158

Calories from Fat: 85

Total Fat: 9.5g

Saturated Fat: 4.8g

Cholesterol: 115mg

Sodium: 64mg

Potassium: 155mg

Total Carbohydrates: 12.5g

Dietary Fiber: 0.9g

Sugar: 1.9g

Protein: 5.8g

Calories: 1424

Calories from Fat: 766

Total Fat: 85.1g

Saturated Fat: 42.8g

Cholesterol: 1031mg

Sodium: 574mg

Potassium: 1394mg

Total Carbohydrates: 113g

Dietary Fiber: 7.8g

Sugar: 17.4g

Protein: 51.9g

39. Carrot Shake

Preparing time: 5 minutes
Servings: 8

1. Ingredients:

300g carrots
200g strawberries
30g parsley
200ml milk
50g coconut milk
30g oats
5 eggs

2. Preparation:

Mix all ingredients in a blender until the composition is smooth.

3. Nutritional facts (amount per 100g/entire composition):

Contains Vitamin A, C, iron, calcium.

Calories: 84

Calories from Fat: 37

Total Fat: 4.1g

Saturated Fat: 2g

Cholesterol: 84mg

Sodium: 64mg

Potassium: 208mg

Total Carbohydrates: 8.2g
Dietary Fiber: 1.7g
Sugar: 3.8g
Protein: 4.4g
Calories: 844

Calories from Fat: 367

Total Fat: 40.8g

Saturated Fat: 20.3g

Cholesterol: 835mg

Sodium: 640mg

Potassium: 2085mg

Total Carbohydrates: 81.7g
Dietary Fiber: 16.5g
Sugar: 37.8g
Protein: 44.2g

40. Grape Shake
Preparing time: 5 minutes
Servings: 8

1. Ingredients:

400g grapes
50g blueberries
200ml milk
100g Greek Yogurt
1 tablespoon vanilla extract
50g whey protein

2. *Preparation:*

Mix all ingredients in a blender until the composition is smooth.

3. *Nutritional facts (amount per 100g/entire composition):*

Contains Vitamin A, C, iron, calcium.

Per 100g	Entire composition
Calories: 88	Calories: 706
Calories from Fat: 12	Calories from Fat: 97
Total Fat: 1.4g	Total Fat: 10.8g
Saturated Fat: 0.8g	Saturated Fat: 6g
Cholesterol: 16mg	Cholesterol: 126mg
Sodium: 29mg	Sodium: 229mg
Potassium: 171mg	Potassium: 1364mg
Total Carbohydrates: 12.2g	Total Carbohydrates: 97.6g
Dietary Fiber: 0.6g	Dietary Fiber: 4.8g
Sugar: 10.8g	Sugar: 86.4g
Protein: 6.9g	Protein: 55.4g

41. Cashew and Cacao Shake

Preparing time: 5 minutes
Servings: 4

1. Ingredients:

50g cashew (chopped)
2 tablespoon cacao powder (30g)
100ml almond milk
200ml water
50g whey protein (chocolate)

2. Preparation:

Mix all ingredients in a blender until the composition is smooth.

3. Nutritional facts (amount per 100g/entire composition):

Contains Vitamin C, iron, calcium.

Calories: 197

Calories from Fat: 127

Total Fat: 14.1g

Saturated Fat: 7.8g

Cholesterol: 26mg

Sodium: 30mg

Potassium: 209mg

Total Carbohydrates: 10.7g

Dietary Fiber: 3.2g

Sugar: 1.9g

Protein: 12.9g
Calories: 789

Calories from Fat: 507

Total Fat: 56.3g

Saturated Fat: 31.3g

Cholesterol: 104mg

Sodium: 119mg

Potassium: 834mg

Total Carbohydrates: 42.9g
Dietary Fiber: 12.7g
Sugar: 7.4g
Protein: 51.7g

42. Kale Shake
Preparing time: 5 minutes
Servings: 6

1. Ingredients:

300g kale
50g parsley
1 lime (juice)
20g ginger
300ml water
50ml milk
50g whey protein

2. *Preparation:*

Mix all ingredients in a blender until the composition is smooth.

3. *Nutritional facts (amount per 100g/entire composition):*

Contains Vitamin A, C, iron, calcium.

Calories: 59

Calories from Fat: 6

Total Fat: 0.7g

Saturated Fat: 0g

Cholesterol: 14mg

Sodium: 36mg

Potassium: 300mg

Total Carbohydrates: 8g
Dietary Fiber: 1.3g
Sugar: 0.8g
Protein: 6.3g
Calories: 475

Calories from Fat: 52

Total Fat: 5.8g

Saturated Fat: 2.6g

Cholesterol: 108mg

Sodium: 288mg

Potassium: 2402mg

Total Carbohydrates: 64.2g
Dietary Fiber: 10.5g
Sugar: 6g
Protein: 50.1g

43.Lettuce Shake

Preparing time: 5 minutes

Servings: 8

1. Ingredients:

300g lettuce
50g spinach
30g parsley
100ml almond milk
30g oats
5 eggs
300ml milk

2. Preparation:

Mix all ingredients in a blender until the composition is smooth.

3. Nutritional facts (amount per 100g/entire composition):

Contains Vitamin A, C, iron, calcium.

Calories: 88

Calories from Fat: 50

Total Fat: 5.5g

Saturated Fat: 3.2g

Cholesterol: 84mg

Sodium: 54mg

Potassium: 172mg

Total Carbohydrates: 5.6g
Dietary Fiber: 0.9g
Sugar: 2.3g
Protein: 4.8g
Calories: 880

Calories from Fat: 498

Total Fat: 55.3g

POST-COMPETITION MEALS FOR BODYBUILDING

BREAKFAST

1. Early Riser Breakfast

Snap your body out of a catabolic state and into a muscle-building one with this high-protein, high-carb oven-cooked breakfast. The grapefruit and asparagus make sure you get more than half a day's worth of vitamin C.

Ingredients (1serving):

6 egg whites

½ cup cooked quinoa and brown rice mix

3 asparagus spears, sliced

½ pink grapefruit

1 small red bell pepper, sliced

1 scoop flavorless whey protein powder

1 clove garlic, crushed

olive oil spray

pepper, salt

Prep time: 10 min

Cooking time: 15-20 min

Preparation:

Heat the oven to 200C fan/ gas 6. Lightly spray a cast iron skillet with olive oil.

In a medium bowl, whisk the egg whites with a pinch of salt and pepper until frothy.

Add the cooked brown rice and quinoa to the skillet; pour in the egg whites then the asparagus pieces and the bell pepper slices.

Bake in the oven for 15-20 min or until the eggs are cooked.

Nutritional value per serving: 407kcal, 52g protein, 40g carbs (5g fiber, 8g sugar), 2g fat, 15% calcium, 12% iron, 19% magnesium, 26% vitamin A, 63% vitamin C, 48% vitamin K, 12% vitamin B1, 69% vitamin B2, 26% vitamin B9.

2. Power Bowl

A breakfast with an appropriate name, the power bowl combines high in protein egg whites with energy fueling oatmeal. The walnuts add healthy fats and the honey tops everything with a bit of sweetness.

Ingredients (1 serving):

6 egg whites

½ cup instant oatmeal, cooked

1/8 cup walnuts

¼ cup berries

1 teaspoon raw honey

Cinnamon

Prep time: 10 min

Cooking time: 5 min

Preparation:

Whisk the egg whites until frothy then cook them in a skillet on low heat.

Combine the oatmeal and the egg whites in a bowl; add the cinnamon and raw honey and mix.

Top with berries, banana and walnuts.

Nutritional value per serving: 344kcal, 30g protein, 33g carbs (3g fiber, 23g sugar), 11g fat (2 saturated), 10% iron, 15% magnesium, 10% vitamin B1, 11% vitamin B2, 15% vitamin B5.

3. Tuna Stuffed Bell Peppers

This is a quick and nutritious recipe that provides a massive amount of B12. High in protein, tuna is an excellent breakfast option for muscle building and if you want to add some carbs to your meal, a piece of whole wheat toast is a great choice.

Ingredients (2 servings):

2 cans of tuna in water (185g), half drained

3 hard-boiled eggs

1 spring onion, finely chopped

5 small pickles, diced

Salt, pepper

4 bell peppers, halved, with the seeds cleaned

Prep time: 5 min

Cooking time: 10 min

Preparation:

Combine the tuna, eggs, spring onion, pickles and seasoning in a food processor and mix until smooth.

Fill the halves of the bell peppers with the composition and serve.

Nutritional value per serving: 480kcal, 46g protein, 16g fat (4g saturated), 8g carbs (2g fiber, 4g sugar), 28% magnesium, 94% vitamin A, 400% vitamin C, 12% vitamin E, 67% vitamin K, 18% vitamin B1, 32% vitamin B2, 90% vitamin B3, 20% vitamin B5, 56% vitamin B6, 18% vitamin B9, 284% vitamin B12.

4. Greek Yogurt with Flaxseeds and Apple

Branch out from the traditional egg white muscle-building breakfast and try some high-protein Greek Yogurt flavored with apple. Use whole flaxseeds to maximize your fiber intake and keep them in water overnight to get them soft and easily digestible.

Ingredients (1 serving):

1 cup Greek yogurt

1 apple, thinly sliced

2 tablespoons flaxseeds

¼ teaspoon cinnamon

1 teaspoon Stevia

A sprinkle of salt

Prep time: 5 min

Cooking time: 45 min

Preparation:

Preheat the oven to 190C fan/ gas 5. Place the apple slices in a non-stick pan, sprinkle them with cinnamon, Stevia and a dash of salt, cover them and bake for 45 min/ until tender. Remove them from the oven and allow them to cool for 30 min.

Place the Greek yogurt in a bowl then top with apples and flaxseeds and serve.

Nutritional value per serving: 422kcal, 22g protein, 39g carbs (7g fiber, 22 g sugar), 21g fat (8 g saturated), 14% calcium, 22% magnesium, 14% vitamin C, 24% vitamin B1, 13% vitamin B12.

5. Bell Pepper Rings with 'Fit Grits'

A tasty and special looking meal, the bell pepper rings with 'Fit Grits' fuel your muscles and give you enough energy to power through your day. Full of color and nutrients, this breakfast is high in vitamin B1.

Ingredients (1 serving):

6 egg whites

2 eggs

¼ cup brown rice farina

1 cup raw spinach

½ green bell pepper

1 cup of cherry tomatoes

Olive oil spray

Salt, pepper

Prep time: 10 min

Cooking time: 15 min

Preparation:

Whisk the egg whites with a pinch of salt and pepper until frothy. Heat some oil in a non-stick frying pan and cook the egg whites and farina. Add the spinach, mix together and cook until the spinach has wilted.

Lightly spray a skillet with olive oil and set on medium heat. Cut the bell peppers horizontally to create 2 rings, place them in the skillet and crack the eggs inside the bell peppers. Let them cook until the eggs turn white.

Place the egg-farina mixture and cooked pepper rings on a plate and serve with cherry tomatoes.

Nutritional value per serving : 495kcal, 45g protein, 45g carbs (3g fiber, 7g sugar), 11g fat (3g saturated), 9% calcium, 14% iron, 20% magnesium, 35% vitamin A, 32% vitamin C, 91% vitamin B2, 22% vitamin B5, 12% vitamin B6, 15% vitamin B12.

6. Almond Milk Smoothie

10 minutes is all you need to fix this high in vitamin D and B1 almond milk smoothie. You can fix a big batch and keep it in the freezer making this smoothie a perfect option for a quick breakfast to go.

Ingredients (2 serving):

1 cup almond milk

1 cup frozen mixed berries

1 cup spinach

1 scoop banana flavored protein powder

1 tablespoon chia seeds

Prep time: 10 min

No cooking

Preparation:

Mix all the ingredients in a blender until smooth, pour into 2 glasses and serve.

Nutritional value per serving: 295kcal, 26g protein, 32g carbs (4g fiber, 13g sugar), 9g fat, 40% calcium, 20% iron, 12% magnesium, 50% vitamin A, 40% vitamin C, 25% vitamin D, 57% vitamin E, 213% vitamin B1, 18% vitamin B9.

7. Pumpkin Pie Protein Pancakes

Forget about flour and try oat pancakes with a delicious addition of fresh pumpkin. Topple some calorie-free syrup and enjoy a high-protein breakfast that tastes as good as a cheat meal.

Ingredients (1 serving):

1/3 cup old-fashioned oats

¼ cup pumpkin

½ cup egg whites

1 scoop cinnamon protein powder

½ teaspoon cinnamon

olive oil spray

Prep time: 5 min

Cooking time: 5 min

Preparation:

Mix all the ingredients together in a bowl. Spray a medium-sized skillet with olive oil then place on medium heat.

Pour in the batter, and once you see tiny bubbles appear on the top of the pancake, flip. When each side is golden, remove the pancake and serve.

Nutritional value per serving: 335kcal, 39g protein, 37g carbs (6g fiber, 1 g sugar), 6g fat, 14% calcium, 15% iron, 26% magnesium, 60% vitamin A, 26% vitamin B1, 37% vitamin B2, 10% vitamin B5, 31% vitamin B6.

8. High-protein Oatmeal

Lasso in a hearty helping of carbs that will keep you satiated for hours, while the protein powder and almonds will deliver a protein-packed start to your day. If you prefer you oatmeal with a fruity taste, use banana flavored protein powder.

Ingredients (1 serving):

2 packets of instant oatmeal (28g packet)

¼ cup ground almonds

1 scoop of vanilla flavored whey protein powder

1 tablespoon cinnamon

Prep time: 5 min

Cooking time: 5 min

Preparation:

Pour the instant oatmeal into a bowl, mix with the protein powder and cinnamon. Add hot water and mix. Top with crushed almonds and serve.

Nutritional value per serving: 436kcal, 33g protein, 45g carbs (10g fiber, 4g sugar), 15g fat (1g saturated), 17% calcium, 19% iron, 37% magnesium, 44% vitamin E, 21% vitamin B1, 21% vitamin B2.

9. Protein-packed Scramble

Feed your muscles and push through an advanced workout with this 51g protein meal. These scrambled egg whites with vegetables and turkey sausage have the added value of being packed with carbs and overall high amounts of vitamins.

Ingredients (1 serving):

8 egg whites

2 link turkey sausages, chopped

1 large onion, diced

1 cup red bell peppers, diced

2 tomatoes, diced

2 cups raw spinach, chopped

1 teaspoon olive oil

salt and pepper

Prep time: 10 min

Cooking time: 10-15 min

Preparation:

Whisk the egg whites with a pinch of salt and pepper until frothy, then set aside.

Heat the oil in a large non-stick pan, drizzle the onions and peppers and sauté until they are tender. Season with salt and pepper. Add the turkey sausage and cook until it is golden brown then lower the heat and add the egg whites and scramble.

When the eggs are almost done, add the tomato and spinach, cook for 2 min and serve.

Nutritional value per serving: 475kcal, 51g protein, 37g carbs (10g fiber, 18g sugar), 10g fat (2g saturated), 14% calcium, 23% iron, 37% magnesium, 255% vitamin A, 516% vitamin C, 25% vitamin E, 397% vitamin K, 22% vitamin B1, 112% vitamin B2, 29% vitamin B3, 19% vitamin B5, 51% vitamin B6, 65% vitamin B9.

10. Fruit and Peanut Butter Smoothie

What better way to get your day's worth of calcium than with this strawberry flavored smoothie? High in minerals, vitamins, protein and energy fueling carbs, this smoothie is a perfect way to kick-start your day.

Ingredients (1 serving):

15 medium-sized strawberries

1 1/3 tablespoons peanut butter

85g tofu

½ cup fat free yogurt

¾ cup skim milk

1 scoop protein powder

8 ice cubes

Prep time: 5min

No cooking

Preparation:

Pour the milk into the blender then the yogurt and the rest of the ingredients. Blend until mixture is completely blended and frothy. Pour into a glass and serve.

Nutritional value per serving: 472kcal, 45g protein, 40g carbs (6g fiber, 31g sugar), 13g fat (4g saturated), 110% calcium, 35% iron, 27% magnesium, 30% vitamin A, 190% vitamin C, 11% vitamin E, 13% vitamin B1, 24% vitamin B2, 10% vitamin B5, 18% vitamin B6, 17% vitamin B9, 12% vitamin B12.

11. Whey Protein Muffins

With a healthy dose of oats and a serving of chocolate whey protein powder, these muffins are a great breakfast alternative to regular oats. Paired with a glass of milk, this meal makes sure that you get a good amount of calcium and vitamin D to go with the nice protein and carbs serving.

Ingredients (4 muffins-2 servings):

1 cup rolled oats

1 large whole egg

5 large egg whites

½ scoop chocolate whey protein powder

olive oil spray

2 cups of low fat milk, to serve

Prep time: 2 min

Cooking time: 15 min

Preparation:

Preheat the oven to 190C fan/ gas 5.

Blend all the ingredients together for 30s. Spray the muffin tin with olive oil then batter up into four muffins. Place in the oven for 15 min.

Remove from the oven, let them cool and serve with the glass of milk.

Nutritional value per serving (includes milk): 330kcal, 28g protein, 37g carbs (9g fiber, 13g sugar), 6g fat (5g saturated), 37% calcium, 22% iron, 19% magnesium, 12% vitamin A, 34% vitamin D, 44% vitamin B1, 66% vitamin B2, 25% vitamin B5, 11% vitamin B6, 24% vitamin B12.

12. Smoked Salmon and Avocado with Toast

Are you in for a tough workout and low on time? It only takes 5 min to piece together this savory breakfast. Both the salmon and avocado are high in healthy acids and this meal has enough protein and carbs to keep you motivated.

Ingredients (2 servings):

300g smoked salmon

2 medium-sized ripe avocados, stoned and peeled

Juice from ½ lemon

handful tarragon leaves, chopped

2 slices of whole wheat bread, toasted

Prep time: 5 min

No cooking time

Preparation:

Cut the avocados into chunks and toss in the lemon juice. Twist and fold the smoked salmon pieces, place them on serving plates, then scatter with the avocado and tarragon. Serve with whole wheat toast.

Nutritional value per serving: 550kcal, 34g protein, 37g carbs (12g fiber, 4g sugar), 30g fat (5g saturated), 17% iron, 24% magnesium, 25% vitamin C, 27% vitamin E, 42% vitamin K, 16% vitamin B1, 24% vitamin B2, 55% vitamin B3, 35% vitamin B5, 40% vitamin B6, 35% vitamin B9, 81% vitamin B12.

13. Breakfast 'Pizza'

Forget about the high-calorie, non-nutritious slice of pizza and replace it with this delicious substitute. Healthy and filling, it only takes 20 min to make and it's not only high in protein, but also in minerals and vitamins.

Ingredients (1 serving):

1 small whole wheat pita

3 egg whites

1 egg

¼ cup low-fat mozzarella cheese

1 spring onion, sliced

¼ cup mushrooms, diced

¼ cup bell peppers, diced

2 slices turkey bacon, chopped

1 teaspoon olive oil

salt and pepper

Prep time: 10 min

Cooking time: 10 min

Preparation:

Whisk the eggs with a pinch of salt and pepper and add the diced vegetables.

Bend the edges of the pita bread to create a bowl. Brush both sides with the olive oil and place the pita bread on the grill, dome side down. Cook until golden then flip it on the other side.

Pour the egg mix into the pita and cook until the eggs are nearly done, add the turkey bacon, spring onion and cheese. Cook until the cheese had melted and serve.

Nutritional value per serving: 350kcal, 33g protein, 12g carbs (3g fiber, 4g sugar), 15g fat (6 saturated), 32% calcium, 19% iron, 15% magnesium, 36% vitamin A, 88% vitamin C, 72% vitamin K, 21% vitamin B1, 71% vitamin B2, 22% vitamin B3, 14%

vitamin B5, 21% vitamin B6, 25% vitamin B9, 29% vitamin B12.

14. Mexican Mocha Breakfast

Top your favorite cup of oats with a healthy serving of almond milk and enjoy a quickly-made high-fiber breakfast. The cayenne pepper is perfect for adding a little oomph to your oatmeal.

Ingredients (1 serving):

½ cup rolled oats

1 scoop chocolate protein powder

½ tablespoon cinnamon

½ teaspoon cayenne pepper

1 cup unsweetened almond milk

1 tablespoon unsweetened cocoa powder

Prep time: 5 min

Cooking time: 3 min

Preparation:

Mix all the ingredients in a microwave-safe bowl. Heat in the microwave for 2 ½ -3 min then serve.

Nutritional value per serving: 304kcal, 27g protein, 38g carbs (8g fiber, 3g sugar), 7g fat, 32% calcium, 15% iron, 25% magnesium, 10% vitamin A, 25% vitamin D, 51% vitamin E, 12% vitamin B1.

15. Blueberry Lemon Pancakes

A warm, filling breakfast, this blueberry pancake enriched by the lemony flavor is a simple and tasty way of getting that high-powered meal that you need to start your day. Spread a tablespoon of Greek yogurt on top of your pancake if you like.

Ingredients (1 serving):

1/3 cup oat bran

5 egg whites

½ cup blueberries

1 scoop flavorless whey protein powder

½ teaspoon baking soda

1 teaspoon grated lemon peel

1 tablespoon lemon drink mix

olive oil spray

Prep time: 5 min

Cooking time: 5 min

Preparation:

Combine all the ingredients in a large bowl, mix and whisk until smooth.

Cook the batch in a sprayed skilled on medium-high temperature until bubbles form on the surface. Flip over and cook until each side is dark golden brown. Remove the pancake and serve.

Nutritional value per serving: 340kcal, 47g protein, 37g carbs (6g fiber, 14g sugar), 5g fat, 10% iron, 25% magnesium, 12% vitamin C, 19% vitamin K, 26% vitamin B1, 58% vitamin B2.

LUNCH

16. Mediterranean Rice

Turn the tired can of tuna into a delicious dish that is a perfect starter for an afternoon of exercise. The high amount of carbs will fuel a thorough workout and the protein will make sure that your muscles recuperate from the effort.

Ingredients (1 serving):

1 can of tuna in oil, drained

100g brown rice

¼ avocado, chopped

¼ red onion, sliced

juice from ½ lemon

salt and pepper

Prep time: 5 min

Cooking time: 20 min

Preparation:

Boil the brown rice for approximately 20 min then place in a bowl with the onion, tuna and avocado. Add the lemon juice and mix all the ingredients. Season with salt and pepper to taste and serve.

Nutritional value per serving: 590kcal, 32g protein, 80g carbs (7g fiber, 1g sugar), 14g fat (5g saturated), 22% iron, 52% magnesium, 101% vitamin D, 18% vitamin E, 107% vitamin K, 32% vitamin B1, 134% vitamin B3, 26% vitamin B5, 39% vitamin B6, 15% vitamin B9, 63% vitamin B12.

17. Spiced Chicken

Chicken is perfect for a high protein muscle building meal. High in nutrients across the board, this simple, tasty meal can be paired with a serving of your choice of carbs.

Ingredients (2 servings):

3 boneless chicken breasts cut in half

175g low-fat yogurt

5cm piece cucumber, finely chopped

2 tablespoons Thai red curry paste

2 tablespoons cilantro, chopped

2 cups raw spinach, to serve.

Prep time: 5 min

Cooking time: 35-40 min

Preparation:

Preheat the oven to 190C fan/ gas 5. Put the chicken in a dish in one layer. Blend a third of the yogurt, the curry paste and two thirds of the cilantro, add salt and pour over the chicken, making sure the meat is evenly coated. Leave for 30 min (or in the fridge overnight).

Lift the chicken onto a rack in a roasting tin for 35-40 min, until golden.

Heat water in a pan and wilt the spinach.

Mix the rest of the yogurt and cilantro, add the cucumber and stir. Pour the mix over the chicken and serve with the cooked spinach.

Nutritional value per serving: 275kcal, 43g protein, 8g carbs (1g fiber, 8g sugar), 3g fat (1g saturated), 20% calcium, 15% iron, 25% magnesium, 56% vitamin A, 18% vitamin C, 181% vitamin K, 16% vitamin B1, 26% vitamin B2, 133% vitamin B3, 25% vitamin B5, 67% vitamin B6, 19% vitamin B9, 22% vitamin B12.

18. Stuffed Eggs with Pita Bread

Get your fill of omega-3 fatty acids with this rich salmon dish. High in vitamins and minerals, this filling meal is a great way of boosting yourself with energy and powering through your day.

Ingredients (2 servings):

1 canned salmon in water (450g)

2 eggs

1 large spring onions, finely chopped

2 large leafs of lettuce

10 cherry tomatoes

1 tablespoon Greek yogurt

a large whole wheat pita bread, cut in half

sea salt and pepper

Prep time: 10 min

Cooking time: 10 min

Preparation:

Boil the eggs, peel them and slice them in half then remove the yolks and place them in a bowl.

Add the canned salmon, 1 tablespoon of yogurt, the spring onion and the seasonings to the bowl. Mix all the ingredients together and stuff the egg whites. Serve with pita bread stuffed with lettuce and tomatoes.

Nutritional value per serving: 455kcal, 45g protein, 24g carbs (3g fiber, 2g sugar), 36g fat (10g saturated), 59% calcium, 22% iron, 21% magnesium, 30% vitamin A, 24% vitamin C, 43% vitamin K, 11% vitamin B1, 36% vitamin B2, 60% vitamin B3, 20% vitamin B5, 41% vitamin B6, 20% vitamin B9, 20% vitamin B12.

19. Chicken Caesar Wraps

These chicken wraps make a great portable meal that will make sure that you keep your protein levels high throughout the day. Throw in some baby spinach and make a more green friendly meal.

Ingredients (1 serving):

85g chicken breast, baked

2 whole wheat tortillas

1 cup lettuce

50g non-fat yogurt

1 teaspoon anchovy paste

1 teaspoon dry mustard powder

1 clove garlic, cooked

½ medium cucumber, chopped

Prep time: 5 min

No cooking

Preparation:

Combine the anchovy paste, garlic and yogurt then toss and coat the lettuce and cucumbers. Split the mix in 2, add to the tortillas and then place half the chicken in each tortilla. Wrap up and serve.

Nutritional value per serving (2 tortillas): 460kcal, 41g protein, 57g carbs (7g fiber, 9g sugar), 10g fat (2g saturated), 11% calcium, 22% vitamin K, 13% vitamin B2, 59% vitamin B3, 12% vitamin B5, 29% vitamin B6, 10% vitamin B12.

20. Baked Salmon with Grilled Asparagus

A classic dish, made more interesting by a marinade of lemon juice and mustard, this grilled salmon goes well with the garlicky asparagus spears. Treat yourself to a great combination of protein and vitamins.

Ingredients (1 serving):

140g wild salmon

1 ½ cup asparagus

Marinade:

1 tablespoon garlic, minced

1 tablespoon Dijon mustard

lemon juice from ½ lemon

1 teaspoon olive oil

Prep time: 5 min

Cooking time: 15 min

Preparation:

Preheat oven to 200C fan/ gas 6.

In a bowl, mix the lemon juice, half the garlic, olive oil and mustard, pour the marinade over the salmon and make sure it is completely covered. Place the marinating salmon in the fridge for at least one hour.

Cut the bottom stems off the asparagus spears. Set a nonstick skillet on medium/high heat, toss the asparagus with the remaining garlic and sear for about 5 min, rolling the asparagus on all sides.

Place the salmon on a baking sheet and bake for 10 min then serve with the grilled asparagus.

Nutritional value: 350kcal, 43g protein, 7g carbs (5g fiber, 1 g sugar), 16g fat (1 saturated), 17% iron, 20% magnesium, 48% vitamin A, 119% vitamin C, 17% vitamin E, 288% vitamin K, 39% vitamin B1, 60% vitamin B2, 90% vitamin B3, 33% vitamin B5, 74% vitamin B6, 109% vitamin B9, 75% vitamin B12.

21. Beef Meatball Pasta with Spinach

A high-protein pasta meal that makes the most of the beef and spinach pairing. Not only is it all-round vitamin packed, but it also contains a hearty amount of magnesium which helps regulate muscle contraction.

Ingredients (2 servings):

For meatballs:

170g lean ground beef

½ cup raw spinach, shredded

1 tablespoon minced garlic

¼ cup red onion, diced

1 teaspoon cumin

sea salt and pepper

For Pasta:

100g wheat spinach pasta

10 cherry tomatoes

2 cups raw spinach

¼ cup marinara

2 tablespoons low-fat parmesan cheese

Prep time: 15 min

Cooking time: 30 min

Preparation:

Preheat oven to 200C/ gas 6.

Mix together the ground beef, raw spinach, garlic, red onion and salt and pepper to taste. Mix thoroughly with your hands until the spinach is completely mixed into the meat.

Form two or three meatballs, roughly the same size then place them on a baking sheet in the oven for 10-12 minutes.

Cook the pasta according to the instructions on the pack. Drain the pasta and stir in the tomatoes, spinach and cheese. Add the meatballs and serve.

Nutritional value per serving: 470kcal, 33g protein, 50g carbs (6g fiber, 5g sugar), 12g fat (5g saturated), 17% calcium, 28% iron, 74% magnesium, 104% vitamin A, 38% vitamin C, 11% vitamin E, 361% vitamin K, 16% vitamin B1, 20% vitamin B2, 45% vitamin B3, 11% vitamin B5, 45% vitamin B6, 35% vitamin B9, 37% vitamin B12.

22. Stuffed Chicken Breast with Brown Rice

Brown rice is an excellent way of introducing quality carbs to your diet. Couple it with high-protein chicken breast and some vegetables and you have a delicious power lunch.

Ingredients (1 serving):

170g chicken breast

½ cup raw spinach

50g brown rice

1 spring onion, diced

1 tomato, sliced

1 tablespoon feta cheese

Prep time: 10 min

Cooking time: 30 min

Preparation:

Preheat the oven to 190C fan/ gas 5.

Slice the chicken breast down the middle to make it look like a butterfly. Season the chicken with salt and pepper, then open it and layer spinach, feta cheese and tomato slices on one side. Fold the chicken breast and use a toothpick to hold it closed then bake for 20 min.

Boil the brown rice then add the garlic and chopped onion. Fill a plate with brown rice, place the chicken on top and serve.

Nutritional value per serving: 469kcal, 48g protein, 46g carbs (5g fiber, 6g sugar), 8g fat (5g saturated), 22% calcium, 18% iron, 38% magnesium, 55% vitamin A, 43% vitamin C, 169% vitamin K, 28% vitamin B1, 28% vitamin B2, 103% vitamin B3, 28% vitamin B5, 70% vitamin B6, 23% vitamin B9, 17% vitamin B12.

23. Shrimp and Zucchini Linguine Pasta Salad

A cheat pasta meal with a serving of shredded zucchini and steamed shrimp flavored with all manners of sesame. This combination of ingredients makes for a light lunch with a high-protein content.

Ingredients (1 serving):

170g steamed shrimp

1 large zucchini, chopped

¼ cup red onion, sliced

1 cup bell peppers, sliced

1 tablespoon roasted Tahini butter

1 teaspoon sesame oil

1 teaspoon sesame seeds

Prep time: 10 min

No cooking

Preparation:

Cut the zucchini using a shredder in order to make raw linguine.

In a bowl, mix tahini and sesame oil.

Place all the ingredients in a large bowl, pour the Tahini sauce and toss it to make sure all sides are covered in sauce. Sprinkle some sesame seeds and serve.

Nutritional value per serving: 420kcal, 45g protein, 26g carbs (10g fiber, 12g sugar), 18g fat (2g saturated), 19% calcium, 47% iron, 48% magnesium, 33% vitamin A, 303% vitamin C, 17% vitamin E, 31% vitamin K, 38% vitamin B1, 36% vitamin B2, 38% vitamin B3, 13% vitamin B5, 66% vitamin B6, 35% vitamin B9, 42% vitamin B12.

24. Turkey Meatloaf with Whole Wheat Couscous

Cooked in a muffin pan, this turkey meatloaf makes sure that you minimize you saturated fats intake. Mix it up a little by adding bell pepper or mushrooms instead of onion into the meatballs and by seasoning with a pinch of ground garlic.

Ingredients (1 serving):

140g lean ground turkey

¾ cup red onions, diced

1 cup raw spinach

1/3 cup low sodium marinara sauce

½ cup whole wheat couscous, boiled

choice of seasoning: Parsley, Basil, Coriander

pepper, salt

olive oil spray

Prep time: 5 min

Cooking time: 20 min

Preparation:

Preheat oven to 200C fan/ gas 6.

Season turkey with your choice of seasoning and add the diced onions.

Light spray your muffin pan with olive oil, place the ground turkey inside the muffin holders. Top each turkey meatball with 1 tablespoon marinara sauce, then place in the oven and bake for 8-10 min.

Serve with couscous.

Nutritional value per serving: 460kcal, 34g protein, 53g carbs (4g fiber, 7g sugar), 12g fat (4g saturated), 12% calcium, 15% iron, 10% magnesium, 16% vitamin A, 15% vitamin C, 11% vitamin E, 16% vitamin K, 11% vitamin B1, 25% vitamin B3, 16% vitamin B6, 11% vitamin B9.

25. Tuna Burger and Salad

The tuna burger is high in protein and carbs, making it an excellent choice for a workout day meal. Fix it differently every time and keep it interesting by switching between vegetables and seasoning your salad dressing.

Ingredients (1 serving):

1 canned chunk tuna (165g)

1 egg white

½ cup chopped mushrooms

2 cups lettuce, shredded

¼ cup dried oats

1 teaspoon olive oil

1 tablespoons low-fat salad dressing (of preference)

small bunch of oregano, chopped

1 whole wheat medium roll cut in half

Prep time: 10 min

Cooking time: 10 min

Preparation:

Mix together the egg white, tuna, dry oats, oregano and form a patty.

Heat the oil in a non-stick pan on medium heat, place the patty on and flip it to make sure it cooks on both sides.

Cut the whole wheat roll in half, horizontally, place the patty between the 2 pieces.

Mix the vegetables in a bowl, add the salad dressing and serve next to the tuna burger.

Nutritional value per serving: 560kcal, 52g protein, 76g carbs (13g fiber, 7g sugar), 10g fat (1g saturated), 11% calcium, 35% iron, 38% magnesium, 16% vitamin A, 16% vitamin K, 35% vitamin B1, 33% vitamin B2, 24% vitamin B3, 28% vitamin B5, 41% vitamin B6, 21% vitamin B9, 82% vitamin B12.

26. Spicy Beefsteak Kebabs

This spicy kebab is served with a side of baked potato, making it not only a muscle building meal but also a great way of introducing eyesight protecting vitamin A to your diet. Add a tablespoon of low-fat yogurt to your potato to make it more refreshing.

Ingredients (1 serving):

140g lean beef flank steak

200g sweet potato

1 bell pepper, chopped

½ medium zucchini, chopped

minced garlic

pepper, salt

Prep time: 15 min

Cooking time: 55 min

Preparation:

Preheat oven to 200C fan/ gas 6. Wrap the sweet potato in a foil, place in the oven and bake for 45 min.

Cut the flank steak into small pieces, season with salt, pepper and garlic. Assemble the kebab, alternating between beef, zucchini and bell pepper.

Place the kebab on a baking sheet and bake for 10 min. Serve with the sweet potato.

Nutritional value per serving: 375kcal, 38g protein, 49g carbs (9g fiber, 12g sugar), 4g fat (1g saturated), 24% iron, 27% magnesium, 581% vitamin A, 195% vitamin C, 21% vitamin K, 22% vitamin B1, 28% vitamin B2, 61% vitamin B3, 28% vitamin B5, 92% vitamin B6, 20% vitamin B9, 30% vitamin B12.

27. Trout with Potatoes Salad

Want to make sure that you are not lacking in vitamin B12? Try this hearty portion of trout, paired with a nutrient and vitamin packed fresh-tasting potato salad.

Ingredients (2 servings):

2*140g trout fillets

250g waxy potatoes, halved

4 teaspoons yogurt

4 teaspoons reduced-fat mayonnaise

1 tablespoon capers, rinsed

4 small cornichons, sliced

2 spring onions, finely sliced

¼ cucumber, diced

1 lemon, zest from ½

Prep time: 10 min

Cooking time: 20 min

Preparation:

Boil the potatoes in salted water for 15 min until they are just tender. Drain and rinse under cold water, then drain again.

Heat the grill.

Mix the mayonnaise and yogurt and season with some lemon juice. Stir the mix into the potatoes with the capers, most of the spring onion, cucumber and cornichons. Scatter the salad with the rest of the onions.

Season the trout, grill on a baking sheet, skin-side down, until just cooked. Scatter with the lemon zest and serve with the potato salad.

Nutritional value per serving: 420kcal, 38g protein, 28g carbs (3g fiber, 6g sugar), 13g fat (3g saturated), 12% calcium, 11% iron, 22% magnesium, 29% vitamin C, 59% vitamin K, 21% vitamin B1, 18% vitamin B2, 12% vitamin B3, 22% vitamin B5, 43% vitamin B6, 18% vitamin B9, 153% vitamin B12.

28. Mexican Bean Chili

A high in protein midday meal, this dish is a great way of getting 1/3 of your daily required amount of fiber. Though it has enough nutrients to be a stand-alone meal, it can also be served on top of a bed of brown rice.

Ingredients (2 servings):

250g minced beef

200g caned baked beans

75ml beef stock

½ onion, diced

½ red pepper, diced

1 teaspoon chipotle paste

1 teaspoon olive oil

½ teaspoon chili powder

1 cup brown rice, boiled (optional)

coriander leaves, to serve

Prep time: 5 min

Cooking time: 45 min

Preparation:

Heat the oil in a non-stick pan over medium heat then fry the onion and red pepper until softened. Increase the heat, add the chili powder and cook for 2 min before adding the minced beef. Cook until browned and all the liquid has evaporated.

Tip in the beef stock, baked beans and chipotle paste. Simmer over a low heat for 20 min, then season and scatter with coriander leaves and serve with the boiled rice.

Nutritional value per serving (without rice): 402kcal, 34g protein, 19g carbs (5g fiber, 10g sugar), 14g fat (5g saturated), 29% iron, 15% magnesium, 42% vitamin C, 11% vitamin B1, 16% vitamin B2, 34% vitamin B3, 40% vitamin B6, 18% vitamin B9, 52% vitamin B12.

½ cup of rice: 108kcal

29. Beef and Broccoli Noodles

A convenient, tasty dish, the beef and broccoli noodles take only 20 min to prepare, making it a great choice for a busy day. You can serve with a few slices of red chili for some extra spice.

Ingredients (2 servings):

2 cups egg noodles

200g beef stir-fry strips

1 spring onion, sliced

½ head broccoli, small florets

1 teaspoon sesame oil

For the sauce:

1 ½ tablespoons low-salt soy sauce

1 teaspoon tomato ketchup

1 garlic clove, crushed

1 tablespoon oyster sauce

¼ knob ginger, finely grated

1 teaspoon white wine vinegar

Prep time: 10 min

Cooking time: 10 min

Preparation:

Mix the ingredients for the sauce. Boil the noodles according to the pack instructions. Tip in the broccoli when they are almost ready. Leave for a few minutes then drain the noodles and broccoli.

Heat the oil in a wok until very hot then stir-fry the beef for 2-3 minutes until browned. Tip the sauce, stir, and let it simmer for a few moments then turn off the heat.

Stir the beef into the noodles, scatter with the spring onion and serve immediately.

Nutritional value per serving: 352kcal, 33g protein, 39g carbs (5g fiber, 5g sugar), 9g fat (2g saturated), 20% iron, 20% magnesium, 20% vitamin A, 224% vitamin C, 214% vitamin K, 14% vitamin B1, 19% vitamin B2, 43% vitamin B3, 18% vitamin B5, 50% vitamin B6, 31% vitamin B9, 23% vitamin B12.

30. Pancetta-wrapped Pollock with Potatoes

This light and fresh-tasting dish provides a lot of energy and is high in protein, making it an ideal option for a midday meal. The pollock can be substituted for another sustainable white fish, while the olives can be replaced by sundried tomatoes.

Ingredients (2 servings):

2* 140g pollock fillets

4 slices pancetta

300g new potatoes

100g green beans

30g kalamata olives

juice and zest from 1 lemon

2 tablespoons olive oil

a few tarragon sprigs, leaves picked

Prep time: 10 min

Cooking time 15 min

Preparation:

Heat oven to 200C fan/ gas 6. Boil the potatoes for 10-12 min until tender, add the beans for the final 2-3 min. Drain well, slice the potatoes in half and tip into a baking dish. Toss with the olives, lemon zest and oil and season well.

Season the fish and wrap with the pancetta then place it on top of the potatoes. Bake for 10-12 min until cooked through, then add the lemon juice, scatter with tarragon and serve.

Nutritional value per serving: 525kcal, 46g protein, 36g carbs (5g fiber, 3g sugar), 31g fat (8g saturated), 10% iron, 31% magnesium, 63% vitamin C, 18% vitamin K, 15% vitamin B1, 13% vitamin B2, 14% vitamin B3, 25% vitamin B6, 73% vitamin B12.

DINNER

31. Sushi Bowl

A low-calorie sushi bowl that substitutes rice for cauliflower flavored with garlic, soy sauce and lime juice for extra taste. Use the seaweed sheets to wrap the veggies and salmon and make a mini roll.

Ingredients (2 servings):

170g smoked salmon

1 medium-sized avocado

½ head cauliflower, steamed and chopped

1/3 cup carrot, shredded

½ teaspoon cayenne

1.2 teaspoon garlic powder

1 tablespoon low-sodium soy sauce

2 seaweed sheets

Juice from ½ lime

Prep time: 10 min

No cooking

Preparation:

Place the cauliflower, carrots, soy sauce, garlic, lime juice and cayenne in a food processor. Stop blending before the mix turns into a paste. Serve next to the salmon and seaweed sheets.

Nutritional value per serving: 272kcal, 20g protein, 13g carbs (7g fiber, 4g sugar), 16g fat (1g saturated), 10% iron, 14% magnesium, 73% vitamin A, 88% vitamin C, 13% vitamin E, 40% vitamin K, 18% vitamin B1, 15% vitamin B2, 31% vitamin B3, 21% vitamin B5, 31% vitamin B6, 26% vitamin B9, 45% vitamin B12.

32. Sweet and Sour Chicken

The sweet and sour chicken is a simple, delicious recipe that has a place in every fit kitchen. It is high in protein and vitamins and goes well with steamed broccoli florets.

Ingredients (2 servings):

300g chicken breasts cut into bite-sized pieces

1 teaspoon garlic salt

¼ cup low sodium chicken broth

¼ cup white vinegar

¼ no-calorie sweetener

¼ teaspoon black pepper

1 teaspoon low-sodium soy sauce

3 teaspoons low-sugar ketchup

arrowroot

400g broccoli florets, steamed

Prep time: 10 min

Cooking time 15 min

Preparation:

Place the chicken in a large bowl and season with the garlic, pepper and salt, turning to coat. Cook the chicken over medium/high heat until done.

In the meantime, whisk together the chicken broth, sweetener, vinegar, ketchup and soy sauce in a sauce pan, bring the mix to a boil and turn to low heat. Add the arrowroot a little at a time and whisk briskly. Keep stirring for a few minutes.

Pour sauce over the cooked chicken and serve with a side of steamed broccoli.

Nutritional value per serving: 250kcal, 40g protein, 14g carbs (6g fiber, 4g sugar), 2g fat, 11% calcium, 14% iron, 20% magnesium, 24% vitamin A, 303% vitamin C, 254% vitamin K, 17% vitamin B1, 21% vitamin B2, 90% vitamin B3, 24% vitamin B5, 58% vitamin B6, 33% vitamin B9.

33. Garlicky Hummus

You only need 5 min to make this healthy, delicious meal. It is chock-full with magnesium and has a decent amount of protein considering the recipe is meatless. Grab a whole wheat tortilla and make this meal to go.

Ingredients (3 servings):

1*400g canned chickpeas (save1/4 of the liquid)

¼ cup tahini

¼ cup lemon juice

1 clove garlic

1 tablespoon olive oil

¼ teaspoon ground ginger

¼ teaspoon ground cumin

2 spring onions, finely chopped

1 tomato, chopped

Prep time: 5 min

No cooking

Preparation:

Place the chickpeas, liquid, tahini, lemon juice, olive oil, garlic, cumin and ginger in a food processor and blend until smooth.

Stir in the tomato and scallions and season with salt and pepper. Serve next to slices of bell pepper.

Nutritional value per serving: 324kcal, 11g protein, 21g carbs (7g fiber, 1g sugar), 17g fat (2g saturated), 22% calcium, 54% iron, 135% magnesium, 10% vitamin A, 12% vitamin C, 33% vitamin K, 122% vitamin B1, 12% vitamin B2, 44% vitamin B3, 11% vitamin B5, 12% vitamin B6, 40% vitamin B9.

34. Chicken with Pineapple and Bell Peppers

Take a break from the usual chicken recipes and try this version with sweet, fresh pineapple. High in vitamin B3 and protein, this meal is also an important source of carbs. In tone with the change of pace, you can substitute the rice for quinoa.

Ingredients (1 serving):

140g boneless chicken breast,

1 tablespoon mustard

½ cup fresh pineapple, diced

½ cup bell peppers, diced

50g brown rice

Coconut oil spray

1 teaspoon cumin

salt and pepper

Prep time: 5 min

Cooking time: 15 min

Preparation:

Cut the chicken into small pieces then rub the mustard on the pieces and season with salt, pepper and cumin.

Set a skillet on medium heat and lightly spray with coconut oil, add the chicken and cook on all sides. When the chicken is almost finished, increase the heat and toss in the pineapple pieces and bell peppers, cook and make sure that all sides are brown. This should take 3-5 min.

Boil the brown rice and serve next to the chicken.

Nutritional value per serving: 377kcal, 37g protein, 50g carbs (6g fiber, 10g sugar), 1g fat, 12% iron, 33% magnesium, 168% vitamin C, 26% vitamin B1, 13% vitamin B2, 96% vitamin B3, 22% vitamin B5, 65% vitamin B6, 10% vitamin B9.

35. Mexican Style Protein Bowl

Give yourself a break from meat and throw these ingredients together for a tasty alternative to the usual. You can skip the fried fat and unhealthy calories and still get the flavor of a Mexican meal.

Ingredients:

1/3 cup cooked black beans

½ cup cooked brown rice

2 tablespoons salsa

¼ avocado, sliced

Prep time: 5 min

No cooking

Preparation:

Combine all the ingredients in a bowl and serve.

Nutritional value per serving: 307kcal, 11g protein, 48g carbs (11g fiber, 1g sugar), 7g fat (1g sugar), 26% magnesium, 13% vitamin K, 16% vitamin B1, 11% vitamin B3, 17% vitamin B6, 30% vitamin B9.

36. Arugula Chicken Salad

The arugula leaves add satisfaction to this sweet and super healthy salad. Bountiful in vegetables and quality protein source, this meal can be enriched with a simple dressing of low-fat yogurt and garlic.

Ingredients (1 serving):

120g chicken breast

5 baby carrots, chopped

¼ red cabbage, chopped

½ cup arugula

1 tablespoon sunflower seeds

1 teaspoon olive oil

Prep time: 10 min

Cooking time: 10 min

Preparation:

Cut the chicken into bite-sized cubes. Heat the olive oil in a non-stick pan and fry the chicken until it is cooked. Set aside and allow cooling.

Place the carrots, arugula and cabbage in a large bowl. Top the salad with the cooled chicken and sunflower seeds and serve.

Nutritional value per serving: 311kcal, 30g protein, 9g carbs (1g fiber), 13g fat (1g saturated), 11% iron, 22% magnesium, 150% vitamin A, 25% vitamin C, 29% vitamin E, 32% vitamin K, 23% vitamin B1, 10% vitamin B2, 72% vitamin B3, 11% vitamin B5, 49% vitamin B6, 17% vitamin B9.

37. Dijon Mustard Halibut

This tangy halibut meal is a fast-and-easy way to get a hearty dose of protein. It's low in carbs and high in vitamins, making it a perfect choice for supper. The low calorie count allows you to double the sauce if you are feeling indulgent.

Ingredients (2 servings):

220g halibut

¼ onion, diced

1 red pepper, diced

1 clove garlic

1 tablespoon Dijon mustard

1 teaspoon Worcestershire sauce

1 teaspoon olive oil

juice from 1 lemon

a bunch of parsley

2 large carrots cut into sticks

1 cup broccoli florets

1 cup mushrooms, sliced

Prep time: 10 min

Cooking time: 20 min

Preparation:

Place the red pepper, garlic, parsley, mustard, onion Worcestershire sauce, lemon juice and olive oil in a food processor.

Place the fish, sauce and the rest of the vegetables in a large parchment baking bag. Bake at 190C fan/ gas 5 for 20 min then serve.

Nutritional value per serving: 225kcal, 33g protein, 12g carbs (3g fiber, 5g sugar), 5g fat (1g saturated), 11% calcium, 10% iron, 35% magnesium, 180% vitamin A, 77% vitamin C, 71% vitamin K, 13% vitamin B1, 19% vitamin B2, 51% vitamin B3, 14% vitamin B5, 34% vitamin B6, 15% vitamin B9, 25% vitamin B12.

38. Tray Bake Chicken

Quick, easy and tasty, this dish should be a summer staple in your kitchen since there is no shortage of fresh cherry tomatoes. The pesto adds a refreshing flavor to a simply seasoned chicken breast.

Ingredients (2 servings):

300g chicken breast

300g cherry tomatoes

2 tablespoons pesto

1 tablespoon olive oil

salt, pepper

Prep time: 5 min

Cooking time: 15 min

Preparation:

Place the chicken breast in a roasting tray, season, drizzle with the olive oil then grill for 10 min. Add the cherry tomatoes and grill for another 5 min until the chicken is cooked. Spread pesto over the top and serve next to the cherry tomatoes.

Nutritional value per serving: 312kcal, 36g protein, 7g carbs (2g fiber, 5g sugar), 19g fat (4g saturated), 15% magnesium, 25% vitamin A, 34% vitamin C, 11% vitamin E, 20% vitamin K, 10% vitamin B1, 88% vitamin B3, 13% vitamin B5, 33% vitamin B6.

39. Tofu burger

Tofu has all of the essential amino acids, and that makes it a perfect substitute for meat. The caramelized onions with chili flakes and Sriracha, paired with the teriyaki infused tofu will delight your taste buds.

Ingredients (1 serving):

85g tofu (extra firm)

1 tablespoon teriyaki marinade

1 tablespoon Sriracha

1 lettuce leaf

30g carrot, shredded

¼ red onion, sliced

½ teaspoon red chili flakes

1 medium-sized whole wheat roll

Prep time: 5 min

Cooking time: 10 min

Preparation:

Heat the grill.

Marinate the tofu in teriyaki marinade, red chili flakes and Sriracha then grill it for 3-5 min on each side.

Fry the red onion in a non-stick pan until caramelized.

Cut the roll in half until you can open it like a book. Stuff the roll with the grilled tofu, caramelized onion, carrots and lettuce and serve.

Nutritional value per serving: 194kcal, 11g protein, 28g carbs (5g fiber, 8g sugar), 5g fat (1g saturated), 21% calcium, 14% iron, 19% magnesium, 95% vitamin A, 10% vitamin B1, 14% vitamin B6.

40. Hot Cod

High in protein and healthy fats and low in carbs, this super spicy cod will give a jolt for the rest of your day. Serve it with a bit of brown rice if you need a carb boost for an evening workout and add 2 more peppers if you feel you can handle more spice.

Ingredients (2 servings):

340g white cod

10 cherry tomatoes, halved

2 jalapeno peppers, sliced

2 tablespoons olive oil

sea salt

chili powder

Prep time: 5 min

Cooking time: 10 min

Preparation:

Heat the oil in a non-stick pan. Coat the cod in salt and chili powder, add to the pan and cook for 10 min on medium heat. Toss in the peppers 1-2 min before the fish is cooked through.

Serve with cherry tomatoes.

Nutritional value per serving: 279kcal, 30g protein, 6g carbs (1g fiber, 1 g sugar), 16g fat (2g saturated), 11% magnesium, 17% vitamin A, 38% vitamin C, 26% vitamin E, 33% vitamin K, 24% vitamin B3, 43% vitamin B6, 26% vitamin B12.

41. Grilled Mushroom and Zucchini Burger

The Portobello mushrooms have a thick, meaty texture that makes them a favorite among vegetarians and meat lovers alike. Indulge in nature's burger and get a load of minerals and vitamins at a minimal calorie cost.

Ingredients (1 serving):

1 large portabella mushroom cap

¼ small zucchini, sliced

1 teaspoon roasted bell peppers

1 slice of low fat cheese

4 spinach leaves

olive oil spray

1 medium-sized whole wheat roll

Prep time: 5 min

Cooking time: 5 min

Preparation:

Heat the grill. Spray the mushroom cap with olive oil then grill both mushroom and zucchini slices.

Cut the roll in half, horizontally, then place the ingredients in layers on one half and cover with the other. Serve immediately.

Nutritional value per serving: 185kcal, 12g protein, 24g carbs (4g fiber, 5g sugar), 4g fat (1g saturated), 21% calcium, 17% iron, 20% magnesium, 78% vitamin A, 28% vitamin C, 242% vitamin K, 15% vitamin B1, 37% vitamin B2, 26% vitamin B3, 16% vitamin B5, 16% vitamin B6, 31% vitamin B9.

42. Mediterranean Fish

What better way to reach your daily B12 requirement than with a dish bursting of Mediterranean flavors? The rest of the vitamins and minerals are also well represented and the protein count is at a good amount for a light supper.

Ingredients (2 servings):

200g fresh trout

2 medium-sized tomatoes

3 teaspoons capers

½ red bell pepper, chopped

1 garlic clove, chopped

10 green olives, sliced

¼ onion, chopped

½ cup spinach

1 tablespoon olive oil

salt and pepper

Prep time: 10 min

Cooking time: 15 min

Preparation:

Heat a large pan over medium heat; add whole tomatoes, garlic and olive oil. Cover and let it simmer for a few minutes until the tomatoes begin to soften.

Add the onion, bell pepper, olives, capers, salt and pepper (and a little water if necessary). Cover and let it simmer until the tomatoes have broken down and the bell pepper and onion have softened.

Add the trout, cover and poach for 5-7 min.

Add the spinach at the last minute then serve.

Nutritional value per serving: 305kcal, 24g protein, 7g carbs (1g fiber, 4g sugar), 11g fat (3g saturated), 10% calcium, 12% magnesium, 36% vitamin A, 56% vitamin C, 62% vitamin K, 13% vitamin B1, 33% vitamin B3, 12% vitamin B5, 25% vitamin B6, 15% vitamin B9, 105% vitamin B12.

43. Vegan friendly dinner

A vegan friendly meal with a good amount of protein and vitamins. Give your palate the taste it deserves with this sweet and spicy sauce that flavors a filling amount of tofu and is easy to make.

Ingredients (2 servings):

340g tofu

¼ cup soy sauce

¼ cup brown sugar

2 teaspoons sesame oil

1 teaspoon olive oil

1 teaspoon chili flakes

2 garlic cloves, minced

1 teaspoon ginger, freshly grated

salt

Prep time: 5 min

Cooking time: 15 min

Preparation:

Mix the brown sugar, soy sauce, sesame oil, ginger, chili flakes and salt in a bowl and set aside.

Pour olive oil into a sauce pan and heat then fry the tofu for about 10 min.

Pour the sauce into the pan and cook for 3-5 min. Serve when the sauce has thickened and the tofu is done.

Nutritional value per serving: 245kcal, 17g protein, 15g carbs (1g fiber, 11g sugar), 15g fat (3g saturated), 34% calcium, 19% iron, 19% magnesium, 11% vitamin B2, 11% vitamin B6.

44. Tuna Melt

Unlike a regular tuna melt that is high in saturated fats and carbs, this one has a moderate amount of carbs and packs the protein-punch of a tuna can, making it an excellent meal that supports lean muscle growth.

Ingredients (2 servings):

1 can of tuna (165g)

2 slices of low-fat mozzarella cheese

2 teaspoons tomato sauce

1 whole wheat English muffin

a sprinkle of oregano

Prep time: 5 min

Cooking time: 3 min

Preparation: 10 min

Preheat the oven to 190C fan/ gas 5.

Slice the English muffin then smear each half with the tomato sauce. Top with the tuna, sprinkle with the oregano and place one slice of cheese on top of the tuna. Place the mini-melts in the oven and bake for 2-3 min or until the cheese has melted then divide between 2 plates and serve.

Nutritional value per serving: 255kcal, 31g protein, 14g carbs (2g fiber, 2 g sugar), 6g fat (4g saturated), 29% calcium, 11% iron, 13% magnesium, 10% vitamin B1, 10% vitamin B2, 60% vitamin B3, 23% vitamin B6, 52% vitamin B12.

45. Chicken with Avocado Salad

A meal that provides a great balance of quality protein and healthy fats that will keep you satisfied without overdoing it on the carbs front. Replace the vinegar with lemon juice for a fresher feel.

Ingredients (1 serving):

100g chicken breast

1 teaspoon smoked paprika

2 teaspoons olive oil

For the salad:

½ medium avocado, diced

1 medium tomato, chopped

½ small red onion, thinly sliced

1 tablespoon parsley, roughly chopped

1 teaspoon red wine vinegar

Prep time: 10 min

Cooking time: 10 min

Preparation:

Heat the grill to medium. Rub the chicken with 1 teaspoon olive oil and paprika. Cook for 5 min on each side until it is cooked through and lightly charred. Cut the chicken in thick slices.

Mix the salad ingredients together, season, add the rest of the olive oil and serve with the chicken.

Nutritional value per serving: 346kcal, 26g protein, 14g carbs (6g fiber, 4g sugar), 22g fat (3g saturated), 16% magnesium, 22% vitamin, 44% vitamin C, 18% vitamin E, 38% vitamin K, 12% vitamin B1, 11% vitamin B2, 66% vitamin B3, 19% vitamin B5, 43% vitamin B6, 22% vitamin B9.

OTHER GREAT TITLES BY THIS AUTHOR

13559676R00208

Printed in Great Britain
by Amazon.co.uk, Ltd.,
Marston Gate.